THE **ANTI-AMERICAN MANIFESTO**

THE ANTI-AMERICAN MANIFESTO

TED RALL

SEVEN STORIES PRESS

NEW YORK

Seven Stories Press
140 Watts Street
New York, NY 10013
www.sevenstories.com

In Canada: Publishers Group Canada, 559 College Street, Suite 402, Toronto, ON M6G 1A9

In the UK: Turnaround Publisher Services Ltd., Unit 3, Olympia Trading Estate,
Coburg Road, Wood Green, London N22 6TZ

In Australia: Palgrave Macmillan, 15–19 Claremont Street, South Yarra, VIC 3141

College professors may order examination copies of Seven Stories Press titles for a
free six-month trial period. To order, visit http://www.sevenstories.com/textbook or
send a fax on school letterhead to (212) 226-1411.

Book design by Jon Gilbert

Library of Congress Cataloging-in-Publication Data

Rall, Ted.
 The anti-American manifesto / Ted Rall. -- 1st ed.
   p. cm.
 ISBN 978-1-58322-933-0 (pbk.)
 1. United States--Politics and government--2009- 2. Revolutions--United States.
I. Title.
 E907.R37 2010
 320.530973--dc22

                          2010031287

Printed in the United States

9 8 7 6 5 4 3 2 1

History doesn't repeat itself; it rhymes.

—Mark Twain

CONTENTS

ACKNOWLEDGMENTS

Thanks to Cole Smithey, Dan Simon, Mary Anne Patey, Bonnie D. Miller, and Merrilee Heifetz. In reverse alphabetical order, because the first shall be last.

A NOTE ON LANGUAGE

It has become standard practice to conflate the citizens and the government of the United States. For instance, even critics of the U.S. government write statements like: "We killed more than a million people in Iraq."

Like the victorious Allies at the end of World War II and Osama bin Laden, I subscribe to the concept of guilt by tacit consent. The United States military would not and could not have killed a million-plus Iraqis if the people who live in the United States had done everything they could to stop them. If Iraqis one day find themselves enjoying the power to hold us accountable for our inaction, they would be right to do so.

However, I do not use "we" to refer to the U.S. government. The government has become so undemocratic and unresponsive that the only reasonable means of opposing it is to strive for its violent overthrow. The revolutionary transformation of an individual from quiescent citizen-poodle to enemy of the state requires a mental separation: the government and its allies in the media and business are not "we the people." They are not even our representatives. They *have murdered more than a million Iraqis. We will stay.* They *must go.*

We who do nothing are complicit.
We who choose to act are not.

KNOW YOUR RIGHTS

The great triumph of Reaganism is that it has convinced Americans to stop demanding that their government do anything for them. This is absurd. Any government, regardless of its political orientation, ought to provide the necessities of life—the things everybody needs to live and thrive—for free. Well, not free—in return for paying taxes. Never forget your ten basic rights:

> Shelter
> Food
> Basic clothes
> Education in accordance with your
>   talents and abilities (through
>   college)
> Medical care
> Retirement benefits
> Transportation
> Communications (telephone, Internet, etc.)
> If you're charged with a crime:
>   competent legal counsel
> In prison: job training and rehabilitation

I. KILL THE ZOMBIE EMPIRE

Governments are instituted among men, deriving their just powers from the consent of the governed . . . Whenever any form of government becomes destructive to these ends, it is the right of the people to alter or to abolish it.

—Declaration of Independence of the United States, 1776

It shall be unlawful for any person with the intent to cause the overthrow or destruction of any government in the United States, to print, publish, edit, issue, circulate, sell, distribute, or publicly display any written or printed matter advocating, advising, or teaching the duty, necessity, desirability, or propriety of overthrowing or destroying any government in the United States by force or violence.

—U.S. Code, from a 1940 law still in effect

You can feel it. Or maybe you can't.

It doesn't matter whether you feel it or not. It's happening. The story of the United States of America as we know it—not merely as the world's dominant superpower, but as a discrete political, economic, and geographic entity—is drawing to a close due to a convergence of emerging economic, environmental, and political crises.

Nothing lasts forever, empires least of all. And this one, which only began to expand in earnest circa the year 1900, doesn't feel like it has the staying power of ancient Rome. Not at all.

But we're not here to talk about the vague possibility of collapse at some point in the future. We are here—in this book and within this historical moment—because the collapse feels as though it is currently in progress.

We are here because the U.S. is going to end soon. There's going to be an intense, violent, probably haphazard struggle for control. It's going to come down to us versus them. The question is: What are you going to do about it?

Definitions:

Us: Hard-working, underpaid, put upon, thoughtful, freedom-loving, disenfranchised, ordinary people

Them: Reactionary, stupid, overpaid, greedy, shortsighted, exploitative, power-mad, abusive politicians and corporate executives

In 2008, like the people of the Soviet Union in the mid-1980s, we put our hopes into a young new leader. He is the kind of fresh-faced reformer who just might have been able to do some good had he been put into power decades ago. "Black Man Given Nation's Worst Job," read the headline in the satirical weekly newspaper the *Onion* after Barack Obama won. He has failed. It is by design that internal reformers like Mikhail Gorbachev and

Obama inevitably come too late to actually accomplish anything. Even if a leader like Obama were inclined to push for the sweeping reforms that might save American late-stage capitalism from itself, as did Franklin D. Roosevelt—and there is no evidence that the thought has crossed Obama's mind—his fellow powerbrokers, fixated on quarterly profit statements and personal position, would never allow it.

The media talks a lot about reform. But it's too late for nips and tucks. Reform can only fix a system if the system is viable and open to change. Neither is true about the United States of America.

A veneer of normalcy slapped—sloppily slapped—on top of a stinking pile of obviously out-of-control unsustainability can no longer disguise the ugly truth: The United States of America is finished. Shopkeepers still take our dollars, foreigners still fear our bombs, but watching the crazy federal deficits, the wildly expanding international military presence, the putrid joke that is our healthcare/education/employment system, and a natural world in free fall (mainly due to the crap pumped into the air and water by the people and corporations of the United States) makes the debate over whether Democrats are better than Republicans feel surreal.

Government exists to serve economic power. In the U.S. and globally, economic power is concentrated in business, namely the large corporations whose profits account for more than ten percent of the nation's gross domestic product.[1] Corporations can't operate without the government. They are codependent, yet independent of and barely responsive to the nation. A nation goes on with or without its government, with or without the big businesses we take for granted. *We* are not the government that serves those companies. *They* are parasites, vampires, hideous monsters that underpay and overcharge us and get fat on the spread. Who are *we* then?

We are their victims. We are weak and pathetic. But only by choice.

We can wait for the system to collapse of its own accord, for the rage of the downtrodden and dispossessed to build, for chaos of some sort to expose and destroy it. But implosion might take a long time. And when it happens, we may find ourselves even more powerless than we are now. They—the hardcore, racist, undereducated, fundamentalist Christian, anti–civil liberties Right—are preparing to step into the breach, to seize power. They can't wait to unleash their venomous hatred on the city-dwelling commie hipster fags they despise. They are armed. They recognize that the system is doomed. They've seen this coming. They're organized and willing to merge their disparate brands of conservatism under a common leadership. Most importantly, they get it. They don't need to be convinced that everything is in play. *They're putting it in play.*

Christian fundamentalists, the millennial end-of-the-worlders obsessed with the Left Behind series about the End Times, neo-Nazi racists, rural black-helicopter Michigan Militia types cut from the same inbred cloth as Timothy McVeigh, allied with "mainstream" gun nuts and right-wing Republicans, have been planning, preparing, and praying for the destruction of the "Godless," "secular" United States for decades. In the past, they formed groups like the John Birch Society and the Aryan Nations. Now the hard Right has a postmodern, decentralized non-organization organization called the Tea Party.

Right-wing organizational names change, but they amount to the same thing: the reactionary sociopolitical force—the *sole* force—poised to fill the vacuum when collapse occurs. The scenario outlined by Margaret Atwood's prescient novel *The Handmaid's Tale*—rednecks in the trenches, hard military men running things, minorities and liberals taken away and massacred, setting the stage for an even more extreme form of laissez-faire corporate capitalism than we're suffering under today—is a fair guess of how a post-U.S. scenario will play out unless we prepare to turn it in another direction.

Although the U.S. has fascist tendencies, it is unlikely that an ascendant American right would embrace fascism in its classic form. But a post-collapse reactionary government would likely have some attributes of fascism. Robert Paxton, who was my history professor at Columbia and is widely regarded as the nation's leading expert on the field, wrote the book on the subject (*The Anatomy of Fascism*). As Professor Paxton told me in 1991, the United States is the nation that is the most likely to go fascist, the one that has the most of the necessary ingredients—including distrust of parliamentary democracy, extreme militarism, and a highly industrialized society—required for a true fascist state. As things stand, there will be no one to prevent this nightmare.

So this book is a call to arms. And an appeal to self-preservation to those who know we can do better.

IF NOT NOW, WHEN?

A war is coming. At stake: our lives, the planet, freedom, living. The government, the corporations, and the extreme right are prepared to coalesce into an Axis of Evil. Are you going to fight back? Will you do whatever it takes, including taking up arms?

History does not really repeat itself. No two historical moments are ever the same. The circumstances that govern a given street corner in Pittsburgh at 8:00 p.m. on December 9, 2011, will never recur.

Yet the motivations and needs of human beings remain constant. There are always parallels with the past, lessons to be learned, bits and pieces that will apply to present and future circumstances. There are even a few eternal truths.

Thinking about the present situation, the historical analogy that best seems to fit the current crisis is the collapse—to be exact, the period shortly before the collapse—of the Soviet Union. The parallels are instructive and scary:

► Overextended empire (U.S. forces currently fighting in Yemen, Pakistan, the Philippines, Colombia, Haiti, plus more than five hundred thousand soldiers and U.S.-funded mercenaries stationed in hundreds of bases around the world)

► Fiscal crisis (skyrocketing national debt owned by foreigners, insane military budget, soaring trade deficits, crash of credit markets, wildly imbalanced tax structure)

► Foreign quagmire (to wit, Afghanistan and Iraq)

► Rising rampant unemployment (unofficial rates over 20 percent)

► Lack of confidence of the citizenry in their government

► Increasingly out-of-touch rulers (government officials talking about economic recovery, declaring recessions over when they never talk about them starting, focusing on bank bailouts when everyone knows it would be more effective to directly help mortgage holders)

► Exceptionalist delusions (the belief that we're too

big, different, and good to fail, which stifles any
attempt to discuss problems)

▶ Widespread apathy (low voter turnout, disinterest
in news and politics, drastically low newspaper
readership but growth of hyperlocal media)

▶ Weak or nonexistent opposition

That last item is where you come in.

You must change that. You must become strong. You
must organize. You must do whatever it takes to oppose
the system. When you get the chance, you must destroy it.

If you don't kill it, it will die nonetheless. But it will drag us
down along with it. That is what happened to the Russians.

Though some Marxist analysts attribute the events of
1991 to counterrevolutionary forces—the politicians who
gathered around Boris Yeltsin certainly fit the bill in some
respects—the Soviet government wasn't actually toppled. It
collapsed. Broke and ideologically exhausted, its adherence
to revolutionary socialist principles having devolved to
mere lip service, the very idea of government as a viable
and necessary entity withered and disappeared. Power
decentralized. Without an organized group of opposition
leaders poised to take the reins, the vacuum was filled by
former factory managers and gangsters who backed the
men who morphed into Russia's present-day oligarchs.
Today Russia is the world's biggest narcostate, a play-
ground for *biznesmeni* (businessmen) and brutal men who

murder journalists and anyone else who criticizes them. Disparity of wealth has soared. A tiny elite, one or two percent of the population, owns everything. There are slot machines in the Moscow metro.

Revolution, though bloody and terrifying, would have been easier than the slow convulsions of collapse. So it will be here.

If the U.S. government is going to collapse anyway, it behooves us to first replace it with something that can stand in its place. Unless we act, we'll have to deal with a post-collapse scenario, in which we'll have to fend off roving criminal gangs, hoodlums, predatory corporations, oppressive residual government entities, and an emboldened political right.

MAD MAX, NOT ECOTOPIA

The enemy is inertia. There are a zillion reasons not to do anything; indeed, we Americans haven't done anything— hell, we haven't *thought* about doing anything—for generations. So, at risk of repeating myself, I must emphasize that our current crisis—economic and political collapse, a surging right poised to take over, with possible environmental apocalypse looming just around the corner—is not going to resolve itself in a way that we like if we sit on our asses. The current U.S. government must be prophylactically removed. Our economic and social structure must be radically reinvented. These things can only happen by using force.

Though small in numbers, anarchists and "deep-green" anticivilization environmentalists are highly influential in what passes for the American Left, publishing well-regarded books, magazines, and blogs that inspire many people. Deep-green types fantasize about a collapse scenario that will save the world without anyone having to lift a finger. They imagine an involuntarily deindustrializing economy that allows the earth to heal while people gather to form small clans and low-impact villages based on ideals of equality. Here is a quote from Jan Lundberg, a deep-green proponent of "peak oil" theory: "New social norms and tribal law will help break from the past and possibly outlaw incipient reversion to the failed system of exploitation of people and nature. In any case, the 'new' model of sharing and cooperation will outdo in productivity any vestiges of the old models of selfishness and trying to insulate oneself or one's family from the surrounding changed world."[2]

That would be nice, but I don't see how the deep-green idyll could logically follow the disintegration of the United States government. Theoretically, people might form intentional communities (the current term for communes) and/or polyamorous clans of one hundred to one hundred fifty in Ecotopia (the term for a theoretical independent Pacific Northwest), living off the land, all local and sustainable-like. But these utopian societies won't be able to count on being left alone to live peacefully. The millions of partisans who follow Fox News, Rush Limbaugh, and right-wing televangelists happen to be the best-armed people around, and they despise just about everyone who doesn't think and pray like them. They will see collapse as affirmation of their beliefs that secular liberalism is destructive. They will also see it as an opportunity to create a new, ordered world atop the ashes. They will act to stop teenage sluts from getting abortions, teach niggers a lesson, and slaughter those spics, dots, and everyone else who doesn't fit into their vision of what and who is right.

Anarchists may opt out of revolution, but counterrevolution will come to them.

Collapse of the U.S. government will be a multidimensional disaster. People, infrastructure, and institutions we count on will be destroyed. How will we live without water treatment plants, heating fuel, and industrially manufactured medicines? What will likely follow will be frightening and even more destructive: post-Soviet-style gangster capitalism, perhaps, warlordism in rural areas, a hard turn to the racist right, even genocide. Doing nothing will seal our doom.

So let's do something. Let's seize power now, before it's too late. Before they (the bad people who are waiting in the wings) do.

If you are old enough to remember the early 1980s, how did you feel when you watched the news and saw Polish workers rise up under the banner of the Solidarity movement? When Chinese students took over Tiananmen Square? When the citizens of Moscow took to the streets to put down a coup by Soviet officials meant to end *perestroika*? When you watched Afghan women burn their *burqas* after the 2001 U.S. invasion that deposed the Taliban? You were probably thrilled. After all, these news stories were presented by U.S. corporate media as officially approved acts of personal and national liberation. And there was some truth to that. These were acts of free will. Of courage. In defense of freedom. You had to have been happy.

I was. I was excited—even though I knew there was less than met the eye to these news accounts. Afghan women, for example, got paid five hundred bucks each by major network television crews to burn their *burqas*. After the B-roll had been shot, they bought new *burqas* for a buck and put them on. I was in Afghanistan at the time, so I know the truth. Yet the power of television is such that I am moved when I watch this (phony) footage. Even though it's bullshit. It's like the statue of Saddam Hussein being pulled down in 2003. It is known that the show at Firdos Square was staged[3] by a U.S. Army "PsyOps" propaganda detachment. The men kicking "Saddam's" head were flown in from exile on U.S. military transports for the occasion; many of them weren't even Iraqi. Nevertheless, images of liberation are always intoxicating.

How do you feel when you hear about a revolution? You

feel good. Oppressors have been toppled, justice has been served, and the people have taken control of their own destiny.

So why not you?

Why not us? Why shouldn't *we* free ourselves? Why shouldn't we seize the mansions and bank accounts of the rich/thieves? Why shouldn't we nationalize corporations? Why can't we take the CEOs who pay themselves millions while firing workers, put them on trial, and throw them in prison? Why shouldn't we bring home the foot soldiers of the military-industrial complex, close the bases overseas, end the wars, and use the resulting peace dividend to build schools and pay teachers decently and heal the sick?

During 2007, 1,350,000 high school students were threatened or injured with a weapon on school property.
—U.S. Centers for Disease Control and Prevention

Why let people in other countries have all the fun/take all the risks? Because the U.S. government is mean? Because its police and soldiers and security apparatus will shoot and beat and jail and ruin anyone and anything that opposes it?

Cowardice is no excuse.

It isn't even viable. In the not-so-long run, taking no action is by far the more dangerous prospect. If we let these bastards continue to screw up our country, our nations, and our natural world, we will die horribly anyway. Those in power are tenacious; if only to save ourselves from their now widely apparent excesses, we must be more determined and persistent and ruthless and violent than they are.

REVOLUTION? THERE'S AN APP FOR THAT

No there isn't. When I showed early drafts of this manifesto to my friends, many asked: What should I *do*? Should I hide in the mountains? Learn how to shoot? Stockpile guns and canned food? Rob a bank? Or should I just live my life, remain alert, and train myself to recognize the revolutionary moment when it comes, so I can spring into action?

I get it, they told me. We're in trouble. We need a revolution. But there aren't any groups to join. *What do you want us to do, Rall?*

Well, that's not what this book is about. I don't want to lead a revolution—not because I'm not willing, but because I wouldn't be good at it. I'm not wired that way. I've never even been a community organizer.

I want to kick people in the ass. To get them thinking. To get *you* thinking. I want you to understand the situation—*your* situation. I want you to see that revolt is a good idea, and that it has never been more necessary. I also want you to size up the opposition (both the government and the extreme right): They will never get weaker. We have as good a chance at taking them on as ever.

I want *you* to lead the revolution—not by giving orders, but by choosing to revolt. Lead, in other words, by taking possession of yourself.

What should you do? Mao said revolution isn't a dinner party, meaning that it's often ugly, violent, and even unjust. I say revolution isn't like joining MoveOn.org or a Facebook group. You don't just click a link and authorize a PayPal donation. Revolution doesn't happen within the system; revolution is the act of destroying the system.

Who are you? That's the first question. What you should do is one thing if you're a taxi driver, something else if you're an accountant who plays in a band on weekends, and something different entirely if you're a kid.

It's not like no one has ever had to figure this stuff out before. When France fell to the Germans in 1940, a significant minority of Frenchmen decided to resist the occupation. But they didn't know what to do, much less who they could trust. There wasn't a Resistance yet. So people went about their business, looking and waiting for a chance to do something. The first step, it turned out, was reaching out to other people. Would neighbors help? Or at least keep quiet? Sometimes the patriots judged incorrectly. Collaborators turned in friends, even members of their own families, to the Gestapo. The stakes were high: torture, death, possibly the murder of their families. Obviously, this isn't Vichy France—but finding allies you can trust is a logical first step.

After they had formed cells, the next step for would-be French resisters was to decide what form their resistance would take. Some Parisian policemen tipped off Jews that they were about to be arrested. Train workers, many of whom were members of the communist labor union CGT, collected intelligence with a view toward passing it along to the Allies. Some women slept with high-ranking Nazi officers in order to collect pillow talk or allow a comrade to kill the officers during sex. In short, people did what they could.

What can you do? That's up to you. You know yourself. I don't. Figure it out.

It seems likely that at this point in history a decentralized organization—a "group" that isn't a group at all, an organization without any leadership whatsoever, a group that is really a set of principles and ideas—stands a better chance of successfully avoiding high-tech government spying and carrying out actions. The Earth Liberation Front, for example, includes among its principles that no humans or animals should be harmed while carrying out an ELF action. There are several other rules. If you follow all of them, congrats! You're "in" ELF. Other contemporary examples of decentralized organizations include the Animal Liberation Front, Al Qaeda, and the Tea Party. Al Qaeda famously allows itself to be "franchised." Though based in Pakistan and Afghanistan, Al Qaeda now has spin-off groups such as Al Qaeda in Mesopotamia (Iraq) and Al Qaeda on the Arabian Peninsula (Saudi Arabia and Yemen). Think of all the Al Qaeda "number two" men who have been killed or arrested since 9/11—Al Qaeda has only grown stronger. That's because personalities don't matter in a decentralized movement. Ideas do. The more a government tries to crush a decentralized resistance organization, the more moderates are radicalized by heavy-handedness. Now we even have the newly identified phenomenon of "self-radicalization," in other words, the process of reading and getting pissed off.

While conducting searches at U.S. borders, federal agents are authorized to take a traveler's laptop computer or other electronic device to an offsite location to analyze its data—even if the traveler is not suspected of wrongdoing.
—*Washington Post*, August 1, 2008[4]

Action is preferable to inaction. But there's always a place for "sleepers"—people who wait until the moment is right to strike. Maybe they want to see the early signs of a mass uprising before committing themselves. Or perhaps they're unwilling to participate directly yet are willing to provide passive assistance—a safe house, say, or financial help or simply looking the other way when something is going down. Part of the revolution may be fought virtually, by hackers. These individuals are every bit as valuable as people who blow stuff up.

Will the United States ever generate a mass movement? Will thousands or even millions of people be willing to commit to militant action against the state? I don't know. I don't think it matters. If everyone waits to see who else is willing to take the chance to resist before resisting himself or herself, no one will resist. As we saw in apartheid-era South Africa, the existence of even small, radical, armed cadres could move the national conversation toward action on the part of millions of others.

I can't hold your hand. I don't want you to buy into everything I say. It's not about me. I don't care if you agree with me. I MAY BE WRONG ABOUT EVERYTHING.

I want you to THINK, dammit! Figure out for yourself what is wrong. Then, once you know what's wrong, don't just grab a beer and veg out, or go to a yoga class, or whatever. Act! Do something about it!

To paraphrase a woman who spent time in prison for her radical activities in the 1960s, once you choose the path of committed citizenship, of true patriotism, of standing up for yourself and your fellow human beings and other living things who can't speak for themselves, your journey can end in only one of three ways: victory, prison, or death.

Then consider the alternative. Once you commit yourself to apathy, laziness, and tacit consent to mass murder and rampant injustice, your miserable, wasteful choice can end only with death.

II. WHY HAVEN'T WE ACTED YET?

I argued in chapter 1 that we must topple the U.S. regime in order to avoid a painful collapse and post-collapse dystopia that would make things worse. Now I want to point out that the anger and misery provoked by the economic crisis presents a unique opportunity to attract support for radical change. The government and its corporate puppetmasters have proven themselves unwilling and unable to soothe the pain of the broad majority of working- and middle-class Americans who have been hit hard by rising unemployment and shrinking wages.

What remains is to break out of our lethargy, to recognize a revolutionary moment in the offing, and to take advantage of it.

The winter of 1944–45 marked the beginning of the end of Nazi Germany. France had been liberated by the Western Allies; the Red Army had pushed Hitler's forces out of western Russia and Eastern Europe. The Thousand Year Reich was crumbling, pressed in on all sides.

The consensus among historians and forensic psychologists is that Adolf Hitler was sane, at least until 1944, when he began popping pills and cracking under the strain of losing the war on both fronts. His regime, on the other hand, was out of its collective mind. As Germany reeled under nightly bombing raids and its territory shrunk by the day, Nazi authorities diverted hundreds of trains desperately needed for troop transports to defend the Reich's shrinking borders. Instead they used this precious rolling stock to ship Jews to concentration and death camps. The killing rate of the Holocaust—which not only served no military purpose, but in fact deprived the regime of soldiers and workers it required for the war effort—reached its zenith at the bitter end, during the last few months of the war.

Crazy, huh?

Perhaps we shouldn't judge the Führer too harshly. After all, he has a few things in common with Barack Obama. (And with us, since we consent to Obama's rule.) Insulated by the famous Beltway bubble, denied access to ordinary citizens and surrounded by "yes men," Obama doesn't have a clue about what's really going on. Like Hitler, Obama continues to squander good life and treasure after bad on wars he can't win.

When it comes to denial, Americans have a lot in common with the people of Germany. The American empire, after all, is at the end of its rope, too.

The problem is primarily financial: a national debt crisis. Deficit hawks have cried wolf about the deficit from FDR to H. Ross Perot, but the numbers have finally hit levels that

threaten the fiscal viability of the federal and state governments. According to government figures at this writing, the
national debt is twelve trillion dollars. Soon a pile of new
debt—numerous short-term credit obligations that will
come due, with interest rates that have nowhere to go but
up—will cause that figure to rise at a spectacular rate. The
interest that has to be paid on it will go up even faster.

In 2009, the federal government paid more than two
hundred billion dollars in interest on government debt. By
2019, debt service will increase to at least seven hundred
billion dollars a year. "In concrete terms," reported the *New
York Times* on November 23, 2009, "an additional five hundred billion dollars a year in interest expense would total
more than the combined federal budgets [in 2009] for
education, energy, homeland security and the wars in Iraq
and Afghanistan."

**Fourteen percent of Americans (about 40 million) are illiterate.
They cannot read a newspaper or user manual.**
—American Human Development Report, 2008–2009[5]

To put these figures in perspective, the federal deficit has
never exceeded 28 percent of gross domestic product. That
28 percent was in 1943, when the United States entered
World War II. Since then, the deficit has never risen above
13 percent of GDP. Here are the percentages for the last

few years. (Notice the negative entry for 2001. We had a surplus! Remember that?)

2001	-1.27% of GDP
2002	1.52
2003	3.47
2004	3.56
2005	2.58
2006	1.90
2007	1.17
2008	3.24
2009	12.93[6]

Due to the confluence of rising interest rates paid on debt and the soaring costs of war, the federal deficit will hit 20 percent of GDP in 2012—and remain there for years.[7]

It was perhaps the most frightening article ever published in the *New York Times*: "Americans now have to climb out of two deep holes: as debt-loaded consumers, whose personal wealth sank along with housing and stock prices; and as taxpayers, whose government debt has almost doubled in the last two years alone, just as costs tied to benefits for retiring Baby Boomers are set to explode."[8]

Like the Nazi bigwigs at the end of a losing war, American politicians and corporate chieftains are largely ignoring this grim financial picture. "What a good country or a good squirrel should be doing," said William Gross, managing director for the Pimco Group bond-management firm in late 2009, "is stashing nuts away for the winter. The United States is not only not saving nuts, it's eating the ones left over from the last winter."

And like the Nazis who thought it was still important to stuff Jews into ovens at the end of the war, the American government is still wasting hundreds of billions of our hard-earned tax dollars killing Muslims—money that might make all the difference were it directed at fixing our wretched economic situation.

According to back-of-the-envelope estimates relied upon by the White House, each U.S. soldier stationed in Afghanistan costs one million dollars a year. So what did President Obama do upon taking office in the middle of the greatest economic catastrophe since the Great Depression? He sent thirty thousand more troops to fight George W. Bush's leftover wars against Iraq and Afghanistan.

Thirty thousand soldiers. Thirty billion additional dollars a year. And for what? To prop up the corrupt and unpopular Afghan puppet regime installed by Bush, to prevent the Taliban from taking power again, and to capture members of Al Qaeda (of whom the Pentagon has said recently that there are only a few dozen left). No matter how you feel about the government, wasting our money—a ton of our money—at a time when we desperately need that money to be spent wisely on the economic crisis affecting the vast majority of Americans here at home—is insane.

There are three takeaways here. Number one: the U.S. government is batshit crazy. Number two: they're robbing us and mortgaging our future—and we're letting them get away with it. Number three: the heedless way they are behaving reveals their weakness. Even when they know what they should be doing to save the system, they can't.

The very nature of the system—the nature of *their* system—requires them to keep sending soldiers to fight losing wars. (All they want to do, argue defense experts, is disrupt potential regional rivals like Iran. But U.S. goals have shrunk in response to U.S. losses.)

They have to fund worthless bankers. If they stopped, it wouldn't be the same system anymore. Obama and other politicians are aware that the American consumer is the golden goose that drives two-thirds of economic spending. They know their inaction on the economy is killing consumer spending and eroding political support for themselves and for the system in general. Like a moth drawn to the flame, they can't help themselves. It's their nature.

THEIR LUNACY IS OUR OPPORTUNITY

Why is the U.S. government digging itself deeper into a fiscal hole from which it will never be able to escape? Because its two principal imperatives, remaining in power and maximizing short-term profit, trump everything else—even its own long-term survival. Because its leaders aren't smart enough to adjust from a period of constant expansion to one of extended contraction. Because politicians refuse to declare war on the businessmen who feed them. Because those businesses make the donations that fund their reelection campaigns. Because the U.S. government is crazy—what could be more insane than refusing to save yourself, no matter who is paying?

And because we don't do anything to stop it.

Thinking about all that government debt can be demoralizing. There's nothing like reading one of those rolling "debt clocks" with lines like: "Your Family's Share: $104,281.17." Chin up! That's just the government trying to vest you in their problem. *They're* broke. You may be broke, too, but not because of the federal debt. All it takes is one little revolution to declare all those Treasury bonds and notes null and void. How many nationalized corporations would it take to get in the black?

The reason we're discussing the federal debt crisis is that it makes a tactical point: namely, the all-powerful U.S. government is hanging on by a slender fiscal thread. They're weaker now than at any point in history. That's good for us. But only, obviously, if we do something about it—namely, take control. If we don't, we really *will* wind up paying back all that money in the form of higher taxes.

When you stop to think about it, it's weird that we put up with governmental malfeasance. America's national mythos and popular culture are permeated with getting even. When a character has been done wrong on television or on film, we've been programmed to expect (violent) payback. Whether it's Charles Bronson gunning down the thugs who raped his daughter and murdered his wife in *Death Wish* or Julia Roberts taking on a company for corporate corruption in *Erin Brockovich*, we like to see the wicked brought low. When an evil corporation or government runs amok, audiences crave the moment of reckoning—e.g., Mussolini and his mistress Clara Petacci hanging from the Esso gas station sign in Milan. In our imaginations, we don't take it. We shoot the bad guys. There's a huge disjunction, though, between our national self-image and our actual day-to-day selves. In real life we settle for so little in the way of fairness, in the way of common sense solutions, in the way of democracy. Why is that?

Whatever happened to the people who live in the land of the "brave and the free"?

Sometimes, when I drive, I wind up behind a long line of slow cars for none of the reasons I consider acceptable: construction, a lane closure, an accident, rush-hour congestion. If you're like me and often in a hurry, you've doubtlessly had a similar experience: There you are, behind a dozen or more cars, driving thirty miles an hour where the legal speed limit is fifty. At the front of this procession is a motorist who, whether oblivious or intentionally inconsiderate, is inconveniencing a lot of people. (Hey, maybe it's an old person who is afraid to drive any faster. Which is fine, but then they ought to pull over to let everyone pass.) Maybe you're three or four cars back. Your anger builds. Not just against the slowpoke, but against the slowpoke's enabler: the second car in line. After all, it's up to the second driver to do something—to flash their high beams or honk. *Do something, asshole.* If car number two can pass, it should—which would set up the third car to try next. But nothing happens. Car number two does nothing. It just drives along, docile, failing its driver's responsibility to express the frustration and concerns of the dozens of motorists behind. Why doesn't the driver of that second car honk? Why don't *we* do anything? Like the driver of car number two, we could do something about our predicament—everyone's predicament—if we chose to. Metaphor over.

ONE HUNDRED THOUSAND ANGRY
NEW YORKERS WITH BRICKS

Every now and then, at times exactly like this, when things turn ugly and people get angry and the rich start to worry that perhaps they've pushed us too far, we get a taste of what would be possible were we to act on our rage. Really: the powerful are scared of us. It's so easy to spook them.

Goldman Sachs, the Wall Street investment bank, was described by the London *Times* as "the best cash-making machine that global capitalism has ever produced." And that was after the economy tanked in 2008. Goldman earned itself a reputation for gluttony even beyond its usual excesses when, with assets of over one trillion dollars, it accepted almost 23 billion dollars in taxpayer bailout funds. Then it turned right around and paid its top executives huge bonuses for their role in helping to destroy the maxed-out financial system.

Americans were furious. "I know I could slit my wrists and people would cheer," Goldman CEO Lloyd Blankfein acknowledged when asked about the outcry. But, Blankfein argued, we were being unfair. Then he displayed the arrogance that had provoked populist anger in the first place. "We help companies to grow by helping them to raise capital. Companies that grow create wealth. This, in turn, allows people to have jobs that create more growth and more wealth. It's a virtuous cycle."

Thus the CEO described the supposed "virtuous cycle" of capitalism that paid him more than fifty million dollars in a single year.

What happened next proves what is possible: anger followed by action. Radio talk show hosts howled in response to another of Blankfein's phrases: "Doing God's work." Newspaper editorial boards scolded. Thousands wrote letters. Even Congress, usually reliably useless, chimed in and threatened to re-regulate the financial markets. Blankfein waited for the storm to blow over, for a distraction—celebrities can always be counted upon to do something dumb. Then something unusual took place—or didn't. The anger didn't fade. Which made Blankfein nervous. So nervous, in fact, that he ultimately had to offer up something like penance—a fund worth half a billion bucks dedicated to the support of small businesses—and an approximation of an apology. "We participated in things that were clearly wrong and have reason to regret," he choked.

It wasn't much, and it sure as hell wasn't enough. Less than a year later, taxpayer-bailed-out Goldman was back at it, issuing its employees an average paycheck of six hundred thousand dollars. "Industry executives acknowledge," the *New York Times* reported in January 2010, "that the numbers being tossed around—six-, seven- and even eight-figure sums for some chief executives and top producers—will probably stun the many Americans still hurting from the financial collapse and ensuing Great Recession."9 Still, the Goldman episode should be instructive to those who can imagine a better world—a world that, among other things, would not include Goldman Sachs. All it took to get the company to loosen their purse strings and change this powerful Wall Street firm's (public) attitude was a little cajoling.

What would a hundred thousand angry New Yorkers armed with bricks (or guns) be able to accomplish? Quite a lot. There sure wouldn't be any more eight-figure bonuses. But many observers think Americans are too comfortable and lazy to rise up.

Lewis Lapham, the former editor of *Harper's* magazine, exemplifies this jaundiced view of We, the People. Writing about the 1960s, Lapham says: "Historians revisiting in tranquility the alarums and excursions of the Age of Aquarius know that Revolution Now was neither imminent nor likely—the economy was too prosperous, the violent gestures of rebellion contained within too small a demographic, mostly rich kids who could afford the flowers and the go-go boots." Lapham wrote that in 2001. Maybe it was accurate then. How about now?

For now, the streets are calm. For now.

Lapham may well have been right about the failure of Americans to revolt when they've had the chance. But there's clearly some aspect of American political culture that explains the absence of a full-fledged revolution for over two centuries. Even during the Civil War, the Confederacy didn't try to depose Abraham Lincoln; it seceded. Anyway, many historians don't consider the American Revolution to be a revolution in a strict sense. One indicator that defines revolution—one set of elites replaces another—didn't happen in 1776. Local elites remained in power. The American Revolution was a war of independence sparked by a tax revolt, not a revolution.

Obviously, U.S. history is full of local upheavals that went national, from Daniel Shea's Whiskey Rebellion to antislavery militant John Brown's abolition movement, to the Civil War draft riots, to anarchists blowing up the New

York stock exchange in 1920, to the Los Angeles riots of the early 1990s that spread to many other major cities. We have also had coups, in effect, brought upon by assassinations such as those of the Kennedys. But those weren't revolutions. We have no tradition of national insurrection, of widespread power struggles in the streets over how we are governed. More often than not, Americans have accepted their lot. We have taken our place in that grim, slow line of cars, internalized the fact that we'll be late to dinner, and ground down our teeth in self-directed frustration.

White Americans have, anyway.

THE BLACK BLOC

"If there is hope," said Winston Smith in *1984*, "it lies with the proles." The consistent, centuries-long, ongoing oppression of African Americans, from slavery to racial profiling by police, represents a fault line in our society that has repeatedly exposed itself in the form of violent, even armed, rebellion. Black Americans have reacted in different ways to their situation. Some have tried to integrate. Others, like Marcus Garvey's black nationalists, the Black Panthers, and (to a lesser extent) Nation of Islam, have opted out of the white-dominant power structure as best they could. Naturally, when blacks have acted against the authorities, most recently in Los Angeles in 1992, they have been brutally suppressed.

Living in New York, I randomly turned on the television one day to find live helicopter footage of angry mobs raging through the streets of South Central Los Angeles. There were rumors of mayhem in midtown Manhattan and other cities. At first I was thrilled. This was it! Revolution! When I learned it was a race riot triggered by police brutality, sadness stepped in. "Not a race riot!" I cried. "What a waste of anger!" Without a coherent assault on the pressure points of state control—media outlets, police stations, government offices—and without widespread support from the majority population, it only took a day or two for the authorities to crush the uprising.

This is the inevitable outcome when a minority group tries to take on the government on its own. Even when the majority dislikes its "leaders" (as now), race-based attacks on the system are doomed to failure. Because the authorities equate the threat to themselves with an existential threat to majority rule, their suppression is especially ruthless. Moreover, uprisings by racial minorities can't rely on broad support from members of other races, especially whites. Even liberal whites, who are otherwise inclined to be supportive, fear that they will be the targets of race-specific outrage. Afraid and paranoid, they will side with the government against minorities they perceive as acting in their own sectarian interest.

Still, the race divide is a major fault line in the U.S., one with deep potential to spark, amplify, or join a whole mess of craziness. Blacks have been denied access to large sections of economic activity, forced into the margins, thrown against obstacles at every turn, and oppressed institutionally for a long time after the end of slavery and since by entrenched political and economic racism. They now rely on racially defined subcultures and networks that white society often characterizes as criminal—which is why they are incarcerated and executed at rates that far exceed either their share of the population or crimes committed. But the rage, and therefore the revolutionary impulse, lives among them.

NOT POOR-POOR, BUT RELATIVELY POOR

In another country, our current economic situation might well have already resulted in violent uprisings among a broad cross-section of races and cultural backgrounds. Working- and middle-class Americans have taken a lot of abuse, especially in terms of their standard of living, since 1973 (when, by the way, average real wages peaked before beginning a decades-long decline).[10]

As conservatives point out, the U.S. isn't Mali or Somalia. Even after decades of declining real wages, living standards in the United States are so much higher than those of the Third World that our poor are better off than their middle class. People's expectations are much lower in those countries than they are here. What drives people to desperation and violence is not some objective set level of deprivation, however, but a relative sense of losing what they value most, of falling behind with little or no prospect of improvement in the future. Americans are furious about economic conditions that the people of Mali and Somalia dream about.

During the last forty-plus years, as two generations have been born and come of age, income has fallen, prices have risen, and jobs have gotten harder to come by. Meanwhile, bosses have become greedier and meaner. In the last few years alone, millions of Americans have been tossed out of the middle class and wound up homeless. Americans aren't rich. Not anymore.

For members of Generations X and Y, born after 1960, the iconic opener of the Port Huron Statement, issued by Students for a Democratic Society in 1962—"We are people of this generation, bred in at least modest comfort"—might as well have been written in Sanskrit. Unlike the Baby Boomers, anger is not a pose for Generations X and Y—and fashion plays little role in their lives of silent seething and brooding alienation.

YES WE CAN, YES WE MUST

If radical change is possible, why hasn't it happened yet? Well, there's fear. Also, people don't know where to begin. The sheer magnitude of the task, which has been carefully cultivated by the system, is immense. "You can't fight City

Hall" has become a mantra of powerlessness in an age of phone mail that doesn't even let you talk to a human being, let alone be heard or exert influence.

If you have a long list of tasks, it's less psychologically daunting if you start with the easy ones and leave the hard ones for later. Similarly, people tend to focus on trying to change the things they think they can affect. They ignore and deny the existence of problems that seem beyond their control—which, these days, is all the big issues. This is at the heart of the "Think Globally, Act Locally" meme. Whether you drive a hybrid or an SUV won't affect global warming. But you can feed the homeless in your community.

Which brings us to the greatest achievement of the American government and its allied corporations, as transmitted through its self-censoring media outlets: It has convinced us that there is nothing we can do about anything.

Progressives/liberals/leftists—whatever we want to call ourselves—we think there's nothing we can do to stop the alarming rate of species extinctions, close the disparity of income and wealth, curb militarism, or just about anything else we care about. Conservatives/libertarians/right-wingers—whatever we want to call them—they think there's nothing they can do to stop abortion, free trade, runaway trade and budget deficits, gun control, or just about anything else they care about. Common ground! Our powerlessness binds us. It could unite us. To be American is to feel helpless.

And yet, not so deep down, we know we are wrong. History proves it. From the English peasants' revolt of 1381 to the uprising and escape of inmates at the Sobibor death camp to the revolution in East Timor, people know what to do when they're oppressed. They get angry. Plot. Rise up. Kill their oppressors. Flee or seize the reins of power. Things change. The history of humanity is the history of struggle. Despite the ludicrous title of Francis Fukuyama's book, history does not end. Nor has history ended merely because we happen to live in America. The old solutions always come back because, in the end, there are no new ones.

SAVE YOURSELF

We, the people of the United States, must rise up because we can't save ourselves any other way. The United States government and the economic system that feeds on it do not serve our interests. To the contrary, the U.S. government is at war with the people of the world who are voiceless due to their geographical separation from the center of power that oppresses them; with the planet, which has been in mortal crisis for many decades; and with its own citizens.

It is time to act!

Why not wait? Why not kick the can down to some future generation—one with more courage? One with deeper despair?

Time costs lives. As time slips away, innocent victims in countries around the world die, the earth heats up, currents stall, species go extinct.

We should free ourselves because we can. Contrary to our social programming and the wishful thinking of those with a vested interest, the U.S. is not immune to the cycles of history. Everything ends. "It simply has not been given to any one society to remain permanently ahead of all the others," wrote Paul Kennedy in *The Rise and Fall of the Great Powers.*

All empires fall. It's only a matter of when and how. And by whom they are destroyed.

We must act. We must dismantle the American Empire. Not someone else. (The Chinese? The EU?) Not some future generation of Americans. We should act now because it will be never be easier to topple this Goliath than now, while it is flailing and broke.

Easier. Not easy. Ridding ourselves of the lattice of powerful, greedy, violent, entrenched special interests who are fucking everything up will be a formidable challenge.

So . . . what if we succeed? What will the future—the American people and our next government—look like?

WHAT NEXT?

I know what I would like the future to look like: more free time, more equality, more focus on keeping people happy and healthy, an end to the state of wage slavery that has condemned us to spend an average of forty-eight hours a week perpetuating a system we hate and increasingly hates us back, and leaders most of us despise. No more wars against countries that have never attacked us. A justice system that treats defendants like people who made mistakes, not blocks of wood to be ground up into dust. A civilization that doesn't rely on an economy that pillages the earth's natural resources and dumps poisons into streams, rivers, lakes, oceans, the air and the ground, even into outer space.

But what I want doesn't matter.

The temptation to plan out the future is understandable. If nothing else, the best marketing tool for revolution is a program. "We cannot reject capitalism," wrote John Strachey in *The Theory and Practice of Socialism*, "unless we have some effective substitute to put in its place. Unless it can be shown that a workable alternative exists, denunciations of the evils of capitalism are vain and empty."[11]

Strachey was wrong. Too many post–World War II revolutionary movements have gotten bogged down in the weeds. Bad institutions, like slavery, don't die until we replace them with something better, as Angela Davis explains in *Abolition Democracy*. First you get rid of the system you hate. Then you create something new.

Besides, that strategy of planning what comes next

before getting rid of what's old is a wasted effort. Revolutionaries never get to lead the revolutionary government. Once one has unleashed long-repressed political and social forces, the situation spins wildly out of control. No one, not even the radicals who worked to make a revolution, can control events. And that's okay. The point of an uprising is not merely to switch out one existing political reality with another, but to alter the political landscape so radically that entirely new ideas, new ways of thinking about and promulgating those ideas, and new leaders rise to the fore.

When one is making the case for revolutionary change, one is not yet making the case for what comes after. Obviously, there will be a successor. A would-be revolutionary should build his case for change based on the utter rottenness of the current regime. Asking a person to support the abolishment of the existing order is asking them to risk everything: their property, their standing in society, their freedom, perhaps even their life. Only a fool would take such a risk on the supposition that it would pay off with an immediate improvement in governance.

Any revolutionary worth her salt should be able to argue that the soon-to-be *ancien régime* is so undeserving of power that it's worth getting rid of it no matter what comes next. Even if it's initially worse.

Remember how optimistic neoconservatives serving in and advising the Bush administration were during the run-up to the 2003 invasion of Iraq? The dictatorship of Saddam

Hussein, they argued, was so brutal and reviled that most Iraqis—certainly the long repressed Shia majority—would welcome "regime change" no matter how it came about. U.S. foreign policymakers assumed that whatever came next would be bound to be an improvement—more democratic, less violent, presumably more pro-American in orientation.

They were mistaken. Iraq turned into a disaster. Soon many Iraqis longed for the days of Saddam. Partly because of the specific failure of U.S. policymakers to do serious planning for the post-invasion period, and more broadly because predicting details on the outcome of social upheaval is difficult even under the best of circumstances, the government that did emerge in post-invasion Iraq has been far less predictable, less functional, and generally far more problematic than most Americans (and most Iraqis) had expected. It also turned out that the Iraqi people did care how regime change came about. They didn't want a government imposed on them from outside, even a democratic one.

Many French revolutionaries living after the overthrow of King Louis XVI rued what followed: the guillotining of tens of thousands of people, including patriots and revolutionaries; the *Directoire*; Napoleon's coup d'état. From there followed one setback after another: military defeats, economic crises, the restoration of the monarchy, the three-year Second Republic that followed the revolution of 1848. It took a full century after the taking of the Bastille for the republican ideals of the revolution to manifest themselves in a national republic with free elections. But what about the alternative? It's hard to imagine that France would have progressed as much politically, that the ideals of liberty, equality, and fraternity would have taken hold had Louis XVI and Marie Antoinette been allowed to die in their beds.

Though born of rational analysis, revolution is a leap of faith—one we must take with care, but without hesitation. Stepping forward blindly—as there is no way to know what will happen next—is the only way to abolish the status quo. The alternative to revolution is insufficient change. And the status quo is unsustainable. It won't last, no matter what we do or don't do. The bubble is bursting. America is getting shittier by the day.

It's ridiculously hard to convince people to risk everything in exchange for the ultimate terror—the unknown. As I mentioned, American history is full of uprisings. In some cases, the repression that followed had the last word. But in others, the repression spread and support came from unexpected quarters. The abolition movement included clergy, slaves, and freed slaves; armed whites acting according to their principles and, in many cases, their religion; and financial support from wealthy individuals or families. The civil rights movement, similarly, had many levels of participants and supporters. Even so these uprisings faced continued stiff resistance that continues to this day. Change came, though not without violence. Without violence, the powerful will never stop exploiting the weak.

Only the possibility that the people will attack and possibly kill their rulers and elite oppressors can keep the latter in check. Fear curbs the excesses of power. But politicians and businessmen will not perceive such a threat as genuine unless the people have actually attacked and sometimes killed them in recent memory. This phenomenon is on display in Western Europe, where two centuries of riot and revolution—occasionally culminating with the executions of ruling elites—keeps those in charge on their toes. During periods of calm, even conservative parties know not to push the people too far. Hard-won social privileges are safer in societies where popular anger bubbles just beneath the surface and occasionally explodes into rage.

However valid, the desirability of curbing the egregious excesses of oppressors is a second reason to chuck the old system. Humanity's eternal quest for happiness drives us to demand the better world that begins with a better country and the full life that can only be had while living in a just and responsive state. A chance for happiness makes life worth living. It is worth risking everything.

WORRY, BE HAPPY

Depressed yet?

Does thinking about crises, crunches, and clampdowns

bum you out (at the morons who let these catastrophes happen)? Are you tired (at the thought of having to struggle and fight)? Me, too. Taking out the trash is never fun. But living in a clean house—well, that's pretty nice. And the chance to move into a nicer place? That's downright thrilling!

Which is what we're talking about. We have lived our entire lives without a chance to really, truly, fundamentally change the things that bother us about our leaders, society, and culture. We live our lives knowing that the world we're born into will be, more or less, the world we die in. We may have made a mark—but we couldn't make a dent. So we've ground our teeth, pinched our faces, and borne countless indignities. We've let assholes run the show in their asshole way.

We are so lucky! We finally have a rare, once-in-a-lifetime opportunity to pursue happiness. Thanks to that most precious of revolutionary resources—populist anger—we can throw out all the rules and start from scratch. Sure, it will be hard and bloody and terrifying. But consider the possibilities: a world, to choose an example at random, without the stupid goddamn fucking insurance companies we have now and where everyone gets medical care! A world without the moronic institution of marriage, an institution nearly everyone hates and almost never really works. A world full of public parks where private golf courses and tennis clubs used to be. Where jobs that don't need to be done can be done away with, where women and men and people of difference races are treated exactly the same and have the same rights, no matter what. A world where people have value, in which they are not treated by employers like crusty snot rags to be thrown away.

What do *you* want? This wasn't true ten years ago, but it is now: *You might actually be able to make it happen.*

You could try to be happy.

Revolution is the quest for happiness. Revolutionaries look around them, see suffering everywhere, and conclude that all that pain and annoyance is unnecessary—that it is so stupid and ridiculous that it is worth throwing out the whole political system and beginning again from scratch. They reject half-assed attempts at reform; why should we settle for being half-happy? Why should a single person suffer unnecessarily?

The purpose of revolution is to abolish unnecessary suffering. The United States in 2010 is a massive case study of people putting up with untold suffering when they shouldn't have to.

The economic collapse is a case in point. Unemployment is higher than it has been at any time since the 1930s. Tens of millions of Americans have lost their homes to foreclosure. Sick people are committing suicide because they can't afford to pay their medical bills.

A paraplegic since a car accident he had suffered as a teen, the singer-songwriter Vic Chesnutt, forty-five,

U.S. Unemployment 1940-2010

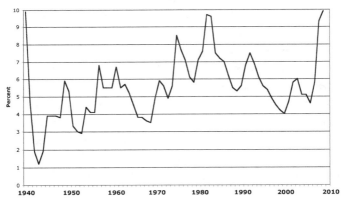

Source: U.S. Bureau of Labor Statistics

despaired of ever being able to pay seventy thousand dollars in medical bills he had accumulated. "I was making payments, but I can't anymore, and I really have no idea what I'm going to do," he said in an interview. "It seems absurd they can charge this much. When I think about all this, it gets me so furious. I could die tomorrow because of other operations I need that I can't afford. I could die any day now, but I don't want to pay them another nickel." And he didn't have to. He committed suicide on Christmas Eve 2009.

On March 6, 2010, an out-of-work Lexus salesman whose home had been foreclosed upon and who could no longer care for his ailing—and uninsured—mother told a real estate agent in New York City he was interested in a high-rise apartment in Queens. When the agent turned his back, Anastasi Calatzis jumped off the terrace.

All this in the richest nation that has ever existed in human history. While billionaires shop for eighth homes and corporations buy profitable companies so they can shut them down and fire their workers. In the United States, poverty is unnecessary. The government could end it overnight. It has chosen not to. It has defended and propped up its true constituents: Wall Street investment banks, commercial banks, and military contractors.

Widespread misery under an unresponsive and uncaring government is a classic recipe for revolution. Yet Americans have not been hungry enough to take to the streets. Perhaps, more precisely, they have not suffered long enough: they have not been so utterly and completely miserable and devoid of hope that they would spend their last dime to buy fuel for a Molotov cocktail. Personal economic downsizing may need to take another steep drop before the fiscal crisis generates a spontaneous riot.

It might take years, even decades, for the country to collapse.

COUNTDOWN TO APOCALYPSE

Even if we're willing to tolerate a long-term deterioration in our standard of living, the planet can't wait.

We face a host of daunting environmental problems: overfishing, air and water pollution, increased viral and bacterial resistance to antibiotics, the massive die-off of bees. The most pressing challenge faced by human beings is global warming caused by greenhouse gas emissions. The U.S. is in a unique position, both as the biggest producer of air-pollution-caused climate change and as a political giant able to use its economic and military muscle to influence other major culprits. In fact, no real progress is possible on the environment without active participation and leadership by the United States. In thrall to businessmen motivated by short-term quarterly profits, American political leaders are doing next to nothing to address this issue. Why, I wonder, are nonhybrid automobiles still legal?

There is no indication that the U.S. government will begin to take global warming seriously absent the overthrow of the nation's political leadership. China recently surpassed the United States as the world's biggest air polluter and emitter of carbon dioxide, the main greenhouse gas. The two countries are in a virtual tie for worst offender. But, per capita, there's no comparison. In 2006, the most recent year for which data is available, the U.S.

belched out 19.78 tons of carbon per capita, compared to 4.58 for China. India, at 1.16, didn't even come close.

If the present rate of anthropogenic climate change continues—a 2008 study commissioned by the National Resources Defense Council concluded that nothing short of an 80 percent reduction in greenhouse gas emissions would slow it down—there will be enormous human, environmental, and economic costs. In 2009 dollars, according to the NRDC, global warming–related expenditures could eventually add up to nearly 2 percent of gross domestic product, or $1.9 trillion annually by 2100. (No one knows for sure. But it will cost a lot.)

Many scientists think the consequences could be more serious than spending a ton of cash: a new ice age à la *The Day After Tomorrow*, the film in which the earth is devastated by disastrous storms, vastly changed coastlines from the much higher sea levels, even global mass extinctions. Most of the world's most productive farmland is predicted to become unarable. As the Arctic first warms and then freezes, even most of the northern hemisphere will burn: a recent government report predicted that average temperatures in the U.S. will increase 11.5 degrees Fahrenheit by 2100.

It may already be too late to save the planet. "Quietly in public, loudly in private, climate scientists everywhere are saying the same thing: it's over," George Monbiot reported in the UK newspaper the *Guardian* from a 2009 climate change summit in Copenhagen. "The years in which more than 2°C [above average temperatures at the start of the Industrial Revolution] of global warming could have been prevented have passed, the opportunities squandered by denial and delay. On current trajectories we'll be lucky to get away with 4°C. Mitigation (limiting greenhouse gas pollution) has failed; now we must adapt to what nature sends our way. If we can."[12]

Ocean levels may rise an average of at least six to sixteen feet by 2100. Good-bye, lower Manhattan. Ciao, south Florida. Bangladesh is toast. The northern half of Antarctica's giant Wilkins ice shelf has begun breaking off; it will be gone within a few years. In the highest mountains in and around the Himalayas, millennia-old glaciers have vanished in the last decade, causing water shortages for hundreds of millions of people in the cities of China and Central and South Asia.

The greenhouse effect is a simple model. The math is straightforward and devastating: so much particulate matter has been pumped into the air since the dawn of the Industrial Revolution two centuries ago, so much energy has built up in the closed system that is our atmosphere that the damage is irreversible. Industrial production has spewed more than two hundred billion metric tons of carbon waste into the atmosphere; we Americans continue to add another six or seven billion annually.

"People have imagined that if we stopped emitting carbon dioxide that the climate would go back to normal in one hundred years or two hundred years," says Susan Solomon, a climate scientist with the National Oceanic and Atmospheric Administration. "What we're showing here is that's not right. It's essentially an irreversible change that will last for more than a thousand years."[13]

Again: It may already be too late, and the time for dithering is past.

Maybe. But maybe not. It is possible that most of the world's scientists are wrong. That climate change isn't really happening. That pollution isn't going to kill us. Not likely, but possible.

And even then—so what? Why not act anyway?

According to NASA, there's a one-in-forty-five-thousand chance that an asteroid called Apophis will strike Earth in 2036. They're long odds—far longer than those for catastrophe caused by climate change. Nevertheless, the Russian Federation has begun a massive project to divert the big space rock and is calling for other countries to pitch in. "We should pay several hundred million dollars and build a system that would allow us to prevent a collision, rather than sit and wait for it to happen and kill hundreds of thousands of people,"[14] said Anatoly Perminov, head of Russia's Roscosmos space agency.

If there's even a 1 percent chance that environmental catastrophe looms, the downside risk is so horrific—even worse than the collision of an asteroid—that we have to do whatever it takes to save ourselves.

The only logical course of action is to do an about-face and change the current course of the U.S. government (which is business as usual), and devote the combined resources and energies of the human race to saving what we can of our planet, its plants, animals, and ourselves.

There is no room in this situation for a system that stands in the way of what must be done. And what must be done is the elimination and drastic reduction of exploitation—of other human beings, other living creatures, and the planet. We cannot succeed entirely, but attempting anything less will inevitably yield the moderate, watered-down, useless "compromises" that are killing us.

Because it is overly concerned with short-term costs and beholden to special interests like big oil companies, the existing political system cannot act decisively. It refuses to dedicate the attention and resources necessary to curb global warming in a meaningful way. A revolutionary war against exploitation is the only way we can begin to directly address and largely solve most of our problems: disparity of income and wealth (not the same thing), environmental degradation, imperialist wars, sexism, racism, homophobia, and so on. Not only would it make us happier, it would save our lives.

REVOLUTION OR COLLAPSE

We can and must avoid a post-Soviet collapse scenario, in

which hundreds of thousands of people starved to death. A post-U.S. collapse would look even uglier than 1991.

Why would a post-U.S. America be worse? In many respects Russians were better prepared for collapse in 1991 than Americans are today. I don't share all of the Russian-American engineer Dmitry Orlov's views, such as his belief that the arrival of "peak oil" production will contribute to a U.S. "hard collapse," as described in his 2008 *Reinventing Collapse: The Soviet Example and American Prospects*. As things stand, energy companies will probably be able to continue pumping old-fashioned dead dinosaur juice out of the ground for hundreds of years to come. But it's harder to dismiss Orlov's succinct observations about the differences between the nation of his birth and his adopted home:

> Poor though it was, the Soviet food distribution system never collapsed completely. In particular, the deliveries of bread continued even during the worst of times, partly because it has always been such an important part of the Russian diet, and partly because access to bread symbolized the pact between the people and the Communist government, enshrined in oft-repeated revolutionary slogans. Also, it is important to remember that in Russia most people lived within walking distance of food shops, and used

public transportation to get out to their kitchen gardens, which were often located in the countryside immediately surrounding the relatively dense, compact cities.[15]

Here in the United States, there is no social safety net for anyone other than the extremely poor, who are only temporarily provided for in the form of welfare and/or unemployment benefits—which would vanish along with the central government. A cowboy culture of "X-treme" individualism has been carefully cultivated in order to make it impossible for a social contract between government and citizenry to spring up in response to our demands. This lone wolf myth is a lie. Most Americans think meat comes wrapped in plastic on Styrofoam trays. They wouldn't know how to kill an animal—assuming they could find one in the melee that would accompany the collapse of industrial agribusiness.

The fragility of America's housing compact would make collapse here particularly brutal. As tough as citizens of the former USSR had it during the 1990s, Orlov reminds us, they didn't have to worry about becoming homeless. "People could not be dislodged from their place of residence for as long as they drew oxygen," he notes. "With several generations living together, families were on hand to help each other." True, after the economy collapsed, people lost their savings, their jobs, those who still had jobs often did not get paid for months, and when they were eventually paid, the value of their wages was destroyed by hyperinflation. But there were no foreclosures, no evictions. As Orlov writes, "Municipal services such as heat, water, and sometimes even hot water continued to be provided, and everyone had their families close by."

Here in the U.S. since 2007, millions of people have already been kicked out of their homes for missing mortgage and rent payments. I say "already" because the U.S. hasn't collapsed yet. If and when it does, we could wind up with bankrupt banks owning all the private houses and apartments, and everyone living outside.

Our nation is sick but eminently savable. Let's not wait until it's on its deathbed before we call a doctor. Rather than wage revolution with a ragged army of formerly middle-class homeless people, let's take over the government, defang the banks, and establish a civil right to housing.

THE CASE AGAINST THE U.S.

There is no moral reason to hesitate. From a moral standpoint alone, it is plain that the world would be better off without the United States government. From its earliest days, U.S. history has been defined by breathtaking acts of violence, exploitation, hypocrisy, colonialism, racism, and genocide carried out in the service of firm policy. Bookshelves groan under the weight of thick volumes cataloguing the endless sins committed by the United States government and, by tacit consent, us.

Over the course of four hundred years, Anglo-American foreign policy has created and expanded one of the most willfully aggressive and genocidal modern nation-states in history, killing and stealing on a scale that rivals Soviet Russia and Nazi Germany. Conservative estimates put the number of Native Americans murdered by British colonists and their American successors at more than ten million people. More recently, American bombs claimed more than two million Vietnamese lives and at least one million Iraqis and Afghans. The United States has covertly propped up scores of vicious dictators around the world who loot their nations' treasuries, brutalize their people, and leave nothing but death and destruction in their wake; it is impossible to count all the victims of such regimes.

Here are two of my standout favorites. Uzbek president Islam Karimov, who receives millions of dollars in direct U.S. funding, is famous in Central Asia for personally supervising massacres and having political dissidents boiled to death. Another is America's next-door neighbor Mexico, whose right-wing dictatorship under Luis Echeverría and José López Portillo kidnapped leftist college students and threw them out of U.S.-supplied military helicopters over the Pacific Ocean during the 1960s and 1970s.

PARTIAL LIST OF U.S. WARS, INVASIONS, AND MILITARY ACTIONS: 1798–PRESENT

Adapted from a List Created by GlobalPolicy.org

DATE	ADVERSARY	ACTION
1798–1800	France	Undeclared naval war against France
1801–1805	Tripoli	First Barbary War, U.S. invasion of Tripoli (Libya)
1806	Spanish Mexico	U.S. Army invades, crossing the Rio Grande for the first of numerous incursions into Mexico
1810	Spanish West Florida	Invasion and seizure of Western Florida, a Spanish possession
1812–1819	Spanish East Florida	Invasion and seizure of Pensacola, Nicholls' Fort, and Amelia Island and adjacent territories. Spain eventually cedes what was then known as the Floridas.
1812–1815	Great Britain	War of 1812
1813	Marquesas Islands	Navy invades and seizes Nukahiva, establishes first U.S. naval base in the Pacific
1815	Algiers and Tripoli	Second Barbary War
1822–1825	Spanish Cuba and Puerto Rico	Marines invade Cuba and Puerto Rico
1827	Greece	Marines invade the islands of Argentiere, Miconi, and Andross
1831	Falkland/Malvinas Islands	Navy invades the Falkland Islands
1832	Sumatra, Dutch East Indies	Navy attacks Qallah Battoo

1833	Argentina	U.S. forces land in Buenos Aires and engage local combatants
1835–1836	Peru	Counterinsurgency operations
1836	Mexico	Invasion and seizure of Texas
1838	Sumatra, Dutch East Indies (now Indonesia)	Punitive expedition
1840–1841	Fiji	Marine invasion
1841	Samoa	Marine invasion
1842	Mexico	Invasion and seizure of Monterey and San Diego
1843	China	Marine invasion of Canton
1843	Ivory Coast	Marine invasion
1846–1848	Mexico	Mexican-American War. Mexico cedes half its territory to the U.S.
1849	Ottoman Empire (Turkey)	Navy dispatched to Smyrna
1852–1853	Argentina	Marines invade Buenos Aires
1854	Nicaragua	Navy bombs and largely destroys city of San Juan del Norte. Marines land and set fire to the remains of the city.
1854	Japan	Commodore Perry and his fleet arrive at Yokohama; forced opening of Japan to external trade
1855	Uruguay	Marines invade Montevideo
1856	Colombia (Panama Region)	Counterinsurgency operation
1856	China	Marines invade Canton
1856	Hawaii	Naval forces seize islands of Jarvis, Baker, and Howland
1857	Nicaragua	Marine invasion

1858	Uruguay	Marine invasion of Montevideo
1858	Fiji	Marine invasion
1859	China	U.S. troops invade Shanghai
1859	Mexico	Invasion of northern Mexico
1860	Portuguese West Africa	Troops invade Kissembo
1860	Colombia (Panama Region)	Navy and Army invasion
1863–1864	Japan	Troops invade Shimonoseki and Yedo
1865	Colombia (Panama Region)	Marines landed
1866	Colombia (Panama Region)	Troops invade and seize Matamoros, later withdraw
1866	China	Marines invade Newchwang
1867	Nicaragua	Marines invade Managua and Leon
1867	Formosa (Taiwan)	Marine invasion
1867	Midway Island	Navy invades and seizes this island in the Hawaiian Archipelago to build a naval base
1868	Uruguay	Marines invade Montevideo
1870	Colombia	Marine invasion
1871	Korea	Invasion
1873	Colombia (Panama Region)	Marine invasion
1874–1893	Hawaii	Navy and marine invasion, seize permanent naval base at Pearl Harbor, overthrow the monarchy
1876	Mexico	Army occupies Matamoros again

1882	British Egypt	Army invades
1885	Colombia (Panama Region)	Army invades Colon and Panama City
1885	Samoa	Navy invasion
1888	Haiti	Army invasion
1888–1889	Samoa	Marine invasion, clash with German navy
1890	Argentina	Navy invades Buenos Aires
1891	Chile	Navy invades Valparaiso
1891	Haiti	Navy invades Navassa Island
1894–1899	Nicaragua	Marines invade Bluefields, Corinto, and San Juan del Sur
1894–1895	China	Marines are stationed at Tientsin and Beijing. A naval ship takes up position at Newchwang.
1894–1905	Korea	Marines invade and seize Seoul
1895	Colombia	Marines invade Bocas del Toro
1898	Puerto Rico, Guam, the Philippines, and Cuba	Spanish-American War. The U.S. invades and seizes an array of Spanish colonies, setting the stage for twentieth-century empire building
1899	Philippines	Beginning of massive counterinsurgency operation by U.S. military, notable for first use of waterboarding and other torture techniques against Filipino patriots
1899	Samoa	Naval invasion

1901–1903	Colombia	Marines invade, land in Bocas de Toro, support "independent coup" separating Panama from Colombia, setting the stage for U.S. dominance of the Panama Canal
1903	Honduras	Marines invade Puerto Cortez
1903	Dominican Republic	Marines invade Santo Domingo
1907–1910	Nicaragua	Joint Army-Navy invasion
1907	Honduras	Marines invade and seize Trujillo, Ceiba, Puerto Cortez, San Pedro, Laguna, and Choloma
1908	Panama	Marine invasion
1911	Honduras	Marine invasion
1912	Panama	Marine invasion
1912	Honduras	Marine invasion
1912–1933	Nicaragua	Marines invade and occupy the country
1913–1916	Mexico	Marines invade Ciaris Estero, seize and occupy port city of Veracruz, cross several hundred miles into Mexican territory in an attempt to put down local revolutionary forces
1914–1924	Dominican Republic	Navy invades Santo Domingo and occupies the country
1914–1934	Haiti	Army invades, bombs, and occupies the country
1917–1918	France	World War I
1917–1933	Cuba	Navy invades, occupies the country

1918–1922	Soviet Union	Navy and Army invade in an attempt to destroy communist revolution
1919	Yugoslavia	Marines invade Dalmatia
1919–1925	Honduras	Marine invasion
1920	Guatemala	Army invasion
1922–1949	China	Navy, Army, and Marines invade, siding with Nationalist forces against communists in Chinese civil war
1932	El Salvador	Naval invasion
1933	Cuba	Naval invasion
1941–1945	Pacific Ocean, Japan, Atlantic Ocean, North Africa, France, Germany, Italy, and many others	World War II. U.S. drops nuclear bombs on Hiroshima and Nagasaki, killing at least one hundred thousand civilians
1946	Iran	Army invasion
1947–1949	Greece	U.S. attempts to defeat Greek revolutionaries
1948	Italy	CIA manipulates national elections
1948–1954	Philippines	CIA "secret war" against local patriots
1950–1953	Korea	Korean War. Attempt to prop up South Korean dictatorship leads to the deaths of at least two million Korean civilians.
1953	Iran	CIA overthrows democratically elected government of Prime Minister Mohammed Mossadegh

1954	Vietnam	Financial and materiel support for colonial French military occupation of Indochina leads eventually to direct U.S. military involvement
1954	Guatemala	CIA overthrows the government of President Jacobo Árbenz Guzmán
1958	Lebanon	Marine and Army invasion
1959	Haiti	Marine invasion
1960	Congo	CIA-backed overthrow and assassination of Prime Minister Patrice Lumumba
1960–1964	Vietnam	Gradual introduction of military advisors and special forces
1961–1962	Cuba	CIA-backed Bay of Pigs invasion, October nuclear missile crisis, and naval blockade
1962	Laos	CIA-backed military coup
1963	Ecuador	CIA backs military overthrow of President José María Velasco Ibarra
1964	Brazil	CIA-backed military coup overthrows the government of João Goulart
1965–1975	Vietnam	Vietnam War. Results in the deaths of between one and two million Vietnamese civilians. Also includes "secret war" against Laos and Cambodia.
1965	Indonesia	CIA-backed army coup overthrows President Sukarno
1965	Congo	CIA-backed military coup overthrows President Joseph Kasavubu

1965	Dominican Republic	Army invasion
1966	Ghana	CIA-backed military coup ousts President Kwame Nkrumah
1966–1967	Guatemala	Counterinsurgency operation
1969	Cambodia	CIA supports military coup against Prince Sihanouk
1970	Oman	Counterinsurgency operation in cooperation with Iranian military
1973	Chile	CIA-backed military coup ousts government of President Salvador Allende
1976–1992	Angola	Military and CIA operations
1980	Iran	Special operations units invade Iranian desert in a failed attempt to rescue U.S. hostages
1981	Libya	Naval jets shoot down two Libyan jets over the Mediterranean
1981–1992	El Salvador	CIA counterinsurgency campaign against local patriots
1981–1990	Nicaragua	CIA directs exile "Contra" death squads against Sandinista government. U.S. air units drop sea mines in harbors, violating international law. Government is eventually deposed.
1982–1984	Lebanon	Marine and Navy invasion
1983	Grenada	Invasion and seizure of Grenada
1984	Iran	Navy shoots down two Iranian fighter jets over the Persian Gulf

1986	Libya	U.S. Air Force bombs Tripoli and Benghazi, including direct strikes on the official residence of President Muamar al Qadaffi. His young adopted daughter is killed.
1986	Bolivia	Counterinsurgency operation against local patriots
1987–1988	Iran	Naval forces block Iranian shipping in the Persian Gulf. Navy shoots down an Iranian civilian airliner.
1989	Libya	Naval aircraft shoot down two Libyan jets over Gulf of Sidra
1989	Philippines	Counterinsurgency operation supports dictatorship over local patriots
1989–1990	Panama	Invasion and seizure of the country. Despite proof of innocence on drug charges, President Noriega is deposed, captured, and imprisoned in the U.S.
1990–1991	Iraq	Gulf War. U.S. drives Iraqi occupation forces out of Iraq, resulting in more than one hundred thousand civilian deaths
1991–2003	Iraq	Continuous bombing of Iraqi targets
1991	Haiti	CIA-backed military coup ousts President Jean-Bertrand Aristide
1992–1994	Somalia	Special operations forces invade, wage war against local warlords
1992–1994	Yugoslavia	NATO blockade of Serbia and Montenegro

1993–1999	Bosnia	U.S. Air Force and Army invades former Yugoslavia
1994–1996	Haiti	Army invades, deposes military rulers and restores President Jean-Bertrand Aristide to office
1995	Croatia	Krajina Serb airfields bombed by U.S. Air Force
1998	Sudan	U.S. air strikes destroy country's major pharmaceutical plant
1998	Afghanistan	U.S. air strikes
2001–present	Afghanistan	U.S. Air Force and Army forces oust Taliban government and install the Northern Alliance, then wage counterinsurgency operations against neo-Taliban and other local patriots
2003–present	Iraq	U.S. forces oust government of Saddam Hussein and establishes puppet government. Occupation force of 150,000 troops plus 300,000 mercenaries engaged in protracted counterinsurgency war against local patriots.
2004	Haiti	Marines land; CIA-backed forces overthrow President Jean-Bertrand Aristide
2005–present	Georgia, Djibouti, Kenya, Ethiopia, Yemen, and Eritrea	War on terrorism. Assassinations and drone plane strikes against civilian targets.
2007	Somalia	Waging airstrikes against the Islamic Courts Union to support the Transitional Federal Government, which controls several blocks in Mogadishu

Under the doctrine of collective responsibility (also called "collective guilt") that the victorious Allies imposed on Germany at the end of World War II, Americans bear collective responsibility for failing to rise up and throw out the series of ruthless presidents whose military adventures and CIA dirty deals have led to global misery, poverty, maiming, and murder. If Germans, who lived in the most extreme totalitarian state ever seen, were to blame for the actions of "their" government, what about us, the citizens of a liberal electoral republic? Even if you don't buy the concept of collective responsibility, consider self-interest: as we witnessed on September 11, 2001, and will see again, a violent and indiscriminately destructive foreign and domestic policy creates "blowback" that kills and maims innocent U.S. citizens on our own soil.

The U.S. government has earned a death sentence with its repeated crimes against its own people, crimes not only of political repression, but also of medical and environmental neglect, racial cleansing, and political persecutions. A 2009 study by the Centers for Disease Control and Prevention found that at least one hundred thousand Americans die annually due to inadequate medical care, mostly due to lack of health insurance. Systemic racism abounds; according to a 1996 study published by the *New England Journal of Medicine*, a black man in Harlem was 4.11 times more likely to die at any given age than the average American white.[16] We witness our government's deadly combination of carelessness and malign neglect during crises like Hurricane Katrina and the swine flu epidemic of 2009. Over 1 percent of American adults are in jail or prison at an annual cost of fifty billion dollars per year. Odds are that you already know most of these things, even if you've never heard of Howard Zinn or Noam Chomsky.

The United States has 2.3 million people behind bars, more than any other nation in the world.
—*Washington Post*[17]

Over 7.3 million people were on probation, in jail or on parole at the end of 2007, equivalent to 3.2 percent of adults.
—U.S. Department of Justice, 2008[18]

One in nine black men aged twenty to thirty-four is in jail.
—*Guardian*[19]

THE WAR AGAINST THE PLANET

U.S.-based and international industrial polluters are waging war against the planet on American soil and around the world, actively and tacitly abetted by federal, state, and local governments. Faux green "lifestyle environmentalists" want us to blame ourselves for not buying enough hybrid cars or recycling our trash, but individual American citizens don't produce nearly as much pollution

as industry and the military. As the deep-green polemicist
Derrick Jensen notes, "Even if every single person in the
United States were to change all their light bulbs to fluo-
rescent, cut the amount they drive in half, recycle half of
their household waste, inflate their tire pressure to
increase gas mileage, use low-flow shower heads and wash
clothes in lower temperature water, adjust their thermo-
stats two degrees up or down depending on the season,
and plant a tree, it would result in only a one-time, twenty-
one percent reduction in carbon emissions."[20]

The U.S. Department of Defense is the world's worst
polluter, belching, dumping, and spilling more pesticides,
defoliants, solvents, petroleum, lead, mercury, and depleted
uranium than the five biggest American chemical corporations combined. According to Steve Kretzmann, director of
Oil Change International, 60 percent of the world's carbon
dioxide emissions between 2003 and 2007 originated in
U.S.-occupied Iraq, due to the enormous amount of oil and
gas required to maintain hundreds of thousands of American military forces and private contractors, not to mention
the toxins released by fighter jets, drone planes, and the
missiles and other ordnance they fire at Iraqis. "The Iraq
war was responsible for at least one hundred forty-one million metric tons of carbon dioxide equivalent (MMTCO2e)
from March 2003 through December 2007," said Kretzmann. "This information is not readily available . . .
because military emissions abroad are exempt from

national reporting requirements under U.S. law and the U.N. Framework Convention on Climate Change."[21]

A 2009 study by the Blacksmith Institute and Green Cross of Switzerland estimates that 40 percent of all human mortality is directly attributable to some form of pollution—smog, sewage, radioactivity, mining, and so on. No one produces more of this toxic waste than the United States (despite having only 5 percent of the world's population). The New York–based Environmental Defense Fund said in 2006 that American-made cars emit the most air pollution, although they only comprise 30 percent of the world's seven hundred million automobiles. Which is by choice: for at least three decades, Detroit automakers have colluded with the federal government to manufacture cars with less than one-fourth of the gas efficiency they were capable of producing.[22] Other nations have repeatedly asked American officials to clean up their act. Unfortunately, the U.S. has stubbornly refused to give in. At the climate change talks in Bali a few years ago, former vice president Al Gore spoke out: "I am not an official, and I am not bound by diplomatic niceties. So I am going to speak an inconvenient truth: my own country, the United States, is principally responsible for obstructing progress here in Bali."

American officials point to China as an example of a country that creates pollution on a scale to rival the U.S. As elsewhere, however, much of the smog over Beijing and other Chinese cities is directly linked to American corporations whose behavior overseas is even worse than at home. Among the twelve top pollution sources in the Chinese capital, for example, are the bottling and distribution factories operated by PepsiCo and Coca-Cola. And China's population is four times bigger.

LOOKING OUT FOR NUMERO UNO

In an attempt to analyze what causes a revolution, Crane Brinton's seminal 1938 study of ferment in the Western world *The Anatomy of Revolution* compared the British revolution led by Oliver Cromwell to the American, French, and Russian revolutions. In France and the Soviet Union, Brinton found that revolutionary fervor was based in the working class. Rage had been there all along. What changed—and made revolution possible—were the sentiments and impulses of people with higher social and financial standing. In both countries, Brinton found that the people who started and/or propelled revolutionary activity had similar motivations during the period leading up to uprisings:

▶ Middle-class and some upper-class individuals who, though not suffering impoverishment—in fact, these revolutions mostly occurred during economic upturns—felt their upward mobility somehow constrained. These are, Brinton wrote, "not-unprosperous people who feel restraint, cramp, annoyance, rather than downright crushing oppression."

▶ Upper-class and some middle-class idealists who have done well for themselves and rue the fact that what they have is not shared by the broad masses. They "have made money, or at least . . . have enough to live on." They "contemplate bitterly the imperfections of a socially privileged aristocracy."

▶ Intellectuals who switch their allegiance from the status quo to ascendant revolutionaries. Whether of opportunistic or idealistic origin, this shift was the most reliable indicator of incipient revolt, argued Brinton.

Revolutionary foment is the group expression of numerous individuals, each motivated by their own peculiar wants, needs, and concerns, acting out in similar ways against those in authority. In other words, the personal is political.

In his 1959 book *The Sociological Imagination*, C. Wright Mills argued that sociology's great promise was that it would analyze personal and psychological issues via the context of politics. The feminist theorist Carol Hanisch coined the phrase "the personal is political" in 1969. There's no doubt that highly personal matters intersect with public policy. For example, countless laws dictate under what circumstances people may engage in sex and what should be done with any resulting progeny. Marriage and divorce are highly regulated. So is schooling. So is dying. And many other obviously personal matters. The role of the state in such matters is a highly charged political situation. And, conversely, taking back personal freedoms from the state is a revolutionary imperative.

SEPARATED AT BIRTH: THE PERSONAL AND THE POLITICAL

In recent years, the average American media consumer has been taught to compartmentalize the personal and the political. Each is assigned its discrete psychological channel. Politics happens on television, on cable news to be exact, and sometimes in newspapers, and also online. Politics has become a spectator sport. Like football. Somewhere far away from the lives and concerns of average Americans toil congressmen and senators and presidents who debate bills and diddle with the tax code. These things, people say, don't have anything to do with them.

Amazingly, politicians admit that they're out of touch with their supposed constituents. They even run campaigns arguing that Washington doesn't care about the people, that we should vote for them because they're less removed from us than those "inside-the-Beltway" politicians they hope to replace—and become.

Political geeks follow these proceedings with great interest. But even they consider politics a "horse race"—not something that affects them personally, every day. I once met Donna Brazile, the Louisianan who managed Al Gore's 2000 presidential campaign and a regular guest pundit on CNN. She could name the elected representative and key political players in any of the nation's 450-plus congressional districts, explain its basic economics and politics, and the prospects for each of the two major parties there. She was a funny and impressive person, and I have no doubt that she was once, and to some extent will always be, motivated by a passionate desire to make the world better. But listening to Brazile discuss the rising and falling fortunes of the Democratic party in Iowa's fifth congressional district struck me as hopelessly irrelevant to the citizenry—even of that district—as it could be.

What does it matter to workers powerless to organize and ask for a raise whether councilperson A or councilperson B—both unable to run unless they pledge fealty to the capitalist system—wins a party primary? In a system dominated by two political parties close together on the political spectrum, it is irrelevant to the man being tortured at a secret CIA prison whether the Democrats or the Republicans control the White House.

American politics aren't politics at all. Politics are the processes that a society engages in as it attempts to determine its beliefs and desires, codify them into legal strictures, and argue about the best way to go about it. American politics are an end in and of themselves. The man or woman who wins is the outcome.

Political campaigns can only result in meaningful improvements in people's lives if the politicians who win them take it upon themselves to spend every waking moment determining what people need and making sure those needs are addressed. In our system, the politician's goal is winning elected office and then holding it—not improving constituents' lives. Our political "leaders" aren't leaders but apparatchiks, dedicating their energies to ensuring their political survival and enhancing their career status to the exclusion of everything else.

Thus our national apathy. We are not bad citizens. We are merely sane. Dumping your bad boyfriend doesn't mean you don't like guys anymore. You still like them. You still like sex. You just want a better boyfriend. Getting rid of your ex gives you time to date.

We no longer care about this political system because it does not serve us. Because it does nothing for us, we are not vested in its survival. We should get rid of it.

We want to know how.

THE POLITICAL IS PERSONAL

Lengthy indictments of governmental offenses against us, our fellow humans, and the earth make infuriating reading. But as the novelist Erich Maria Remarque (not Stalin) wrote: "The death of one man is a tragedy. The death of a million is a statistic." Thus the column-inch mention of a flood in China is drowned out by millions of words and billions of broadcast seconds expended on the latest baby to tumble down a well. Individual stories resonate; general overviews do not. One may or may not think this is bad. No matter. This is how our chimpanzee brains are wired.

In 1969 it meant something to state that the personal is political. Today, we need to be reminded that the political is always personal.

Injustices caused by government are not abstract. To the contrary, they destroy countless human lives. Many serve as indictments that amplify and accelerate how much Americans hate their elected representatives and the institutions of government that are highly responsive to a few elites, but not to us.

Back to the historian Crane Brinton. Revolution becomes seen as necessary, he writes, when "the governmental machinery is clearly inefficient, partly through neglect, through a failure to make changes in old institutions."[23]

Read each of the following three 2009 news stories. The first is about an almost certainly innocent man executed by the state of Texas. The second concerns a community in West Virginia where drinking water is killing people, particularly children. The third relates the tale of a woman pushed into homelessness over a ten-dollar car inspection sticker. All are heartbreaking. Each one functions as a parable for a society equally unable and unwilling to address its problems.

You will probably feel angry and helpless as you read them—the helplessness of empathy. You may not have paid as high a price as the people in these three cases. But you have surely suffered something similar, albeit less severely. If you've ever been falsely accused yet unable to get justice, if you've ever worried about suffering physical harm because some company cut corners to make a few bucks, if you've ever taken a financial hit due to the irresponsibility of a corporate executive you never met, if you've ever sat on hold and tried to get through to someone and realized that no, there just wasn't anything you could do, that you were fucked, fucked, fucked—well, you see where we're going with this. We're all in this together.

Except for those who are doing it to us. They're not in it with us.

The suffering is their fault.

The pain is their idea.

CASE I: The Railroaded Dirtbag

Innocent people have been executed as long as capital punishment has existed. It's different, however, when it happens in the United States. The claim that we live in a nation of laws, where justice ultimately prevails—truth, justice, and the American way, as comic books link them—is drilled into American schoolchildren.

Few other countries brag as much about their judicial systems. Even among some of the liberal democracies of Europe, defendants are presumed guilty until proven innocent.

For hundreds of years, it had been an article of faith that no innocent person has ever been executed in the United States. At the very least, no one could prove otherwise. That changed in 2009. After the case of Todd Willingham came to national attention, Innocence Project co-director Barry Scheck said, "There can no longer be any doubt that an innocent person has been executed."

If even one innocent person has been executed, the death penalty is ipso facto morally bankrupt. But I am not here to discuss capital punishment. I am here to discuss insanity. The state of the nation is nuts.

What is notable about this case isn't the high probability that an innocent man was murdered by the state. The interesting thing about Todd Willingham's journey to the gurney where he was executed is that the system worked—mostly—yet he was killed anyway.

Journalists championed his case. A state review board decided in his favor. Prosecutors, police, and one of the nation's leading arson experts said his life should be spared. Officials from across the political spectrum came out against Willingham's execution.

Willingham's case attracted the interest of the Innocence Project, a group of law students and senior lawyers who find capital cases they believe to have been miscarriages of justice. The Texas Board of Pardons and Paroles eventually agreed to review the case. Governor Rick Perry even agreed to consider commuting his sentence.

Willingham may well have been guilty. We will never know what happened in a rundown house in a hardscrabble backwater of Texas in December 1991. But, in a sane society, Willingham would never have been convicted, much less executed. The doubts were too great. Too many influential people and institutions opposed his death.

But ours is not a sane society. Capital punishment is a runaway train, careening down the track to certain doom. Vengeance, rather than justice, is the obsession of a criminal prosecutorial system that fights prisoners who ask for new DNA tests.

Despite years of appeals, the hard work of talented attorneys, and the interest of the media, Willingham was doomed—by his class, his personal history, and force of circumstance. If the United States was ever a nation based on the rule of law, it isn't anymore.

Two days before Christmas Day 1991 Todd Willingham woke up to the smell of smoke and the sound of his three daughters—a two-year-old and a pair of one-year-old twins—screaming. "My babies are burning up!" he shouted to a neighbor as the blaze spread. Firefighters blocked Willingham from entering the house. "We had to wrestle with him and then handcuff him, for his and our protection," one later recalled. "Based on what I saw on how the fire was burning, it would have been crazy for anyone to try and go into the house," said another.

Influenced by the fact that Willingham was something of a dirtbag—he had hit his girlfriend, the mother of the three girls, when she was pregnant—police and fire investigators in Corsicana, Texas, soon concluded that he had set the fire with the intention of killing his daughters. The fact that Willingham's feet were unburned proved instrumental in the authorities' assessment. Two weeks later, they filed charges.

"The children were interfering with his beer drinking and dart throwing," sniped the local district attorney.

As is often the case in capital murder cases in Texas, in which the defendant is forced to rely upon a court-appointed lawyer, the trial went quickly and badly. A jailhouse snitch testified that Willingham had confessed to the crime to him while he languished behind bars, too poor to make bail. Some witnesses claimed that he hadn't acted as distraught as one would expect of a father who had just lost all his kids. Then there were the fire experts, who said the blaze was an open-and-shut case of arson.

Even Willingham's lawyer thought he was guilty. "All the evidence showed that he was one hundred per cent guilty. He poured accelerant all over the house and put lighter fluid under the kids' beds," the attorney said.

The prosecutor poured it on. In an interview with ABC, district attorney John Jackson claimed that Willingham had killed his kids as part of a ritualistic human sacrifice to Satan. His evidence: Willingham listened to heavy metal music and had a metal poster in his house. The fire patterns on the floor—supposedly the result of arson—were in the shape of a pentagram.

But the prosecutor wasn't as certain as he claimed in public. To the surprise of Willingham's attorney, the state offered life in prison in exchange for a guilty plea. Willingham refused. "I ain't gonna plead to something I didn't do, especially killing my own kids," he insisted.

Willingham spent twelve years on death row. They were eventful years for *Texas v. Willingham*; the prison informant recanted his story, and a respected arson expert, who reviewed the findings of the high-school-educated team whose testimony had sent Willingham to prison, declared the team's analysis "junk science."

It didn't do any good.

Texas, after all, is one of many states where politicians have long found that coming off as "tough" on the death penalty is a surefire vote getter. (George W. Bush, who signed more than one hundred death warrants as governor and never commuted a single sentence, reportedly allocated less than twenty minutes to consider the guilt or innocence of each condemned inmate.) After they strapped Willingham to the gurney that would become his deathbed, he uttered his last words: "The only statement I want to make is that I am an innocent man convicted of a crime I did not commit. I have been persecuted for twelve years for something I did not do."

Noted fire scientist Craig Beyler, employed by a state board established to review cases of forensic errors in 2005, believes Willingham. "In a scathing report," wrote *The New Yorker* magazine, "[Beyler] concluded that investigators in the Willingham case had no scientific basis for claiming that the fire was arson, ignored evidence that contradicted their theory, had no comprehension of flashover and fire dynamics, relied on discredited folklore, and failed to eliminate potential accidental or alternative causes of the fire."[24]

Even the initial investigators never saw the supposed burn patterns. So much for the human sacrifice angle.

The late Todd Willingham was poised to become the first person acknowledged by a modern judicial system in the United States to have suffered the "execution of a legally and factually innocent person."[25]

Then Governor Perry stepped in.

Less than forty-eight hours before Beyler was scheduled to testify before the Texas Forensic Science Commission, Perry fired the chairman and two other members of the commission, replacing them with close political allies. The new chairman canceled the Willingham hearing. Beyler was told his testimony would not be required. At this writing, a few newspapers have issued mildly negative editorials. But nothing has changed. Obviously, nothing can bring Willingham back. He is still classified as a child murderer. And no one has been inconvenienced for their role in his conviction.

CASE 2: Love That Dirty Water

Seventeen miles outside Charleston, West Virginia, residents are suffering the effects of contaminated groundwater. Decade after decade, coal companies dumped arsenic, barium, lead, manganese, and other chemicals into the soil with impunity, ignoring warnings that resulting toxicity levels were high enough to cause cancer and damage kidneys and the central nervous system of humans.

Ten years ago the locals began noticing evil smells coming out of their taps. Children got rashes and scabs after taking baths. Dentists reported the disintegration of tooth enamel in patients who used tap water to brush their teeth. People of all ages came down with gall bladder diseases, fertility problems, miscarriages, chronic stomach ailments, and kidney and thyroid issues—classic signs of severe environmental contamination.

Lawsuits have been filed. The Environmental Protection Agency has been summoned. But nothing much has changed. According to Nixon- and Reagan-era EPA chief William Ruckelshaus, this is because the public isn't angry enough. "When we started regulating water pollution in the 1970s, there was a huge public outcry because you could see raw sewage flowing into the rivers. Today the violations are much more subtle—pesticides and chemicals you can't see or smell that are even more dangerous," he said. "And so a lot of the public pressure on regulatory agencies has ebbed away."[26] To be sure, the ongoing trend of deregulation that began with Reagan and continued through Clinton and both Bushes, had a role, as did the reduction in EPA staffers assigned to enforcement. But apathy allowed these things to happen, too.

Meanwhile, the *New York Times* quotes Jennifer Hall-Massey, whose family has been devastated by the waterborne pollutants left behind by the rapacious mining companies. "How can we get digital cable and Internet in our homes, but not clean water?" she asks. The answer, of course, is that cable television and high-speed Web access is something we pay for, whereas water is a free or heavily subsidized service provided to most Americans. The accounts receivable departments of health insurance companies and cable television companies are well staffed and have modern equipment. Someone answers the phone; you don't have to wait on hold. It's not quite the same thing when you file a claim.

CASE 3: Sticker Shock

"There but for the grace of God go I," goes the saying, but most of us don't believe it. Middle-class Americans—middle-class white

Americans—think that if they keep their heads down, follow the rules and work hard, they'll be okay. In a nation with few social safety nets, that was never true. Now, as millions suffer downward class mobility, the truth is undeniable: no one is safe.

Dorothy Thomas was driving her 1996 Toyota Corolla when a San Jose police officer ordered her to pull over. The cop noticed that Thomas didn't have a current vehicle registration sticker. When he ran her plates through the police computer system, he learned that this was the second time she had been ticketed for not having an auto registration sticker. Following procedure, he called into headquarters to have the car towed away.

"I got down on my knees and begged the officer," she remembers.

The cost of the sticker was ten dollars.

But Thomas no longer had a ten-dollar problem. Now she needed hundreds of dollars to extract her car from the tow pound. The longer the city kept her car, the more debt from various fees she incurred. In the end, she owed sixteen hundred dollars. She lost her car. Without a car, Thomas couldn't commute to her job in the administrative offices of a local hospital in mass-transit-unfriendly California. Without a paycheck, she couldn't pay rent. Within a year, she ended up homeless.

PLEASE PRESS "9" FOR MORE OPTIONS

A rigid, unresponsive, and uncaring system does not serve those that it should serve: the people. Modern-day allegories tell of a society that has stopped making sense. They are symptoms of a system too ossified to fix itself. They are not singularities.

Most indictments of our legal, economic, and political systems focus on the most extreme cases of abuse and neglect. Surely, it can reasonably be argued, a country that legalized torture, as the United States did beginning in 2001, and whose citizens don't seem particularly agitated about it, is morally corrupt. Tens of thousands of Muslim men vanished from the streets of American cities after September 11, 2001. Some have no doubt been permanently "disappeared." The horrors of Abu Ghraib, Guantánamo Bay, and the Bagram air base in Afghanistan and the relative lack of a response by the American public tell the same story about us that Auschwitz and Dachau did about Germany under the Nazis. Of course Muslims are not the only targeted group in twenty-first-century America. Other favorite targets: African-Americans, Latinos, gays, immigrants, and on and on.

Of course, no government is perfect. Officials make mistakes of judgment, of timing. Screw-ups are normal. Citizens understand. They don't expect perfection. But Americans seem to expect it less than any other nationality. "It may not be a perfect system," says one Mayan to another in a cartoon by Tim Kreider as they witness two priests extracting the beating heart of a victim of human sacrifice, "but it's still the best one there is." Millions of people live under superior forms of government now—in Europe and Scandinavia, for example.

But most Americans don't know about the alternatives. Most never travel overseas. Before he became president in 2001, George W. Bush—the scion of a wealthy Connecticut family and a graduate of Yale and Harvard—had never held a passport. The same is true of most Americans. If you have never seen anything else, it is difficult to visualize a different way.

From a historical perspective, the most reliable indicator of a regime's viability is not the level of freedom it accords its subjects. It is its responsiveness. One of the advantages enjoyed by totalitarian states is an often-ignored aspect of their intrusiveness into the everyday minutiae of people's lives. In China, for example, local block cadres and "neighborhood ladies" track visitors to their neighbors' homes. They're aware of citizens' problems, complaints, and concerns. In this way it is possible for an incompetent or corrupt local official to be reported by an otherwise submissive citizenry and for widespread concerns—a plant whose billowing smokestacks generate air pollution that causes asthma among children or stagnant salaries—to come to the attention of provincial officials and, when necessary, officials in Beijing. The system doesn't always work. If the authorities are wise, they will act to address people's concerns. If they are not, they risk provoking one of the rebellions that has punctuated the turnover of dynasties that have lasted thousands of years.

A relatively open society such as the one currently prevailing in the United States offers the ruling class the chance to gauge public opinion cheaply and easily. Scientific polling, news reports, letters to the editor, blogs, and public protests are some of the ways leaders can monitor the mood of the masses. Yet presidents, governors, and congressmen are usually clueless. Pundits blame the "bubble" of security and insularity that surrounds public officials for their separation from the concerns of ordinary people. Veteran politicians complain that they suffer from information overflow—with so many interest groups competing for their attention, they feel psychologically flooded. But who speaks for the people?

Five months after taking office, *U.S. News & World Report* reported that Obama was "doing all he can to stay connected" to the concerns of ordinary Americans. But the paucity of his supposed efforts was pathetically revelatory. These included meeting with a group of presidential historians, "holding town-hall meetings with citizens, reading 10 letters from Americans each day, and having as normal a family life as possible by spending lots of time with his wife, Michelle, and two daughters, Malia and Sasha."[27]

If our society wants to vest as much power in one individual as we have in the president, which is moving our country toward the status of a totalitarian state, the only way such a country can function effectively is for its leader to be more in tune with the masses than any president in American history—certainly more than Obama. No matter how much time Obama spends with his daughters or reading letters from ordinary citizens, he has neither the inclination nor the natural empathy to respond to needs that are rapidly approaching crisis dimensions.

Nonresponsive rulers rule at their own peril. And when threatened, they seem to become even less responsive. So again, who speaks for the people?

KICK 'EM WHILE THEY'RE DOWN

On Christmas Day 1993 I stood next to my mother in front of a war memorial in Pleubian, a small town in Brittany. Listed before us were the names of relatives who had died in France's recent wars: the Franco-Prussian War of 1870, the two World Wars, Indo-China, and Algeria. "Nothing," my mother said. "They all died for nothing."

No one wants to die—especially not a meaningless death. Vince Lombardi aside, winning isn't all that matters. Whether in football or politics, victory is never assured. On the other hand, failure is guaranteed to those who don't make the attempt. As for revolutionaries who try but fail, they should know that their efforts are not in vain.

Even when a government survives a challenge to its authority, the mere fact of said challenge—when it is startlingly powerful—sometimes proves to be a mortal blow to an unjust regime in the long run.

The Indian rebellion against the imperial forces of the British Raj in 1857 is a classic example. The Sepoy Mutiny, as it was called at the time, was bloodily suppressed the following year, and the Brits continued to rule over India for another century. But the Sepoys didn't die for nothing. The fact that the uprising occurred at all, as well as its unexpected (though short-lived) success inspired generations of nationalists living in British colonies to plan revolts of their own. If the mighty British Empire could be forced to step back for a full year, mulled these visionaries, perhaps it could be kicked out entirely. Eventually, it was.

AMERICA'S FOUR CHERNOBYLS

The accidental meltdown at the Chernobyl nuclear power plant was a signature event in the decline and fall of the Soviet Union. When the vast scale of the catastrophe and its cause (poor design and dysfunctional organization) became public, the regime was exposed as incompetent. In addition, in a state where maintaining power relied on the ability to keep secrets, the fact that the disaster became public knowledge indicated impotence. If the regime couldn't cover up such events, perhaps it wasn't logical to fear it. In hindsight, Chernobyl marked the beginning of the end.

Ironically, it has since become known that the Soviet

government didn't try to cover up Chernobyl. Victims of a Moscow version of the Beltway bubble, the central authorities simply didn't know what was going on. "We spent the first days trying to get the picture," Gorbachev said twenty years later. "I can't agree that we were trying to conduct a sly policy and hide something."[28] Public perception, rather than reality, proved pivotal.

We all know the four events that defined the presidency of George W. Bush. We won't know the facts behind the scenes in the corridors of power until archives are declassified. Insofar as they were reported by the news media and are widely understood by American citizens, however, these four disasters exposed several facets of decline simultaneously: political corruption, professional ineptitude, and military and economic impotence:

▶   A majority of Americans believe that the presidential election of 2000 was stolen and a usurper sat in the highest seat of power in the land for eight years.

▶   A majority of Americans also believe that 9/11 could have been prevented if our military, our intelligence community, or our elected officials, not to mention the bureaucracy at American and United airlines, had been even halfway competent. And a substantial minority, here and around the world, believes it was a put-up job.

▶ Most Americans now know that we went to war with Iraq based on lies told to us by our president and members of his cabinet about Iraq having an active program developing weapons of mass destruction.

▶ Most Americans now know that the biblical destruction wrought upon the great city of New Orleans by Hurricane Katrina could easily have been avoided by better planning, and that the loss of life and wholesale destruction that occurred in the aftermath could easily have been avoided by an even modestly effective federal disaster response effort.

PSEUDO-DEMOCRACY EXPOSED

To liberals and others who remained fully vested in the system, these four events prompted dismay and confusion. To others—the American regime's foreign enemies and Americans who dream of a better way of living, governing, and being governed—these events demonstrated that American power, far from being monolithic and undefeatable, was worm eaten and feeble. In merely eight years, each of the U.S. government's fundamental ideological underpinnings had crumbled away.

The myth of America as a vibrant democracy to be emulated by developing countries has endured almost since the beginning of American democracy. "Our country has always been exceptional," write Richard Lowry and Ramesh Ponnuru in a typical example that ran in the *National Review*. "It is freer, more individualistic, more democratic, and more open and dynamic than any other nation on earth."[29] Of course, this is laughable on its face: with its two major parties close together on the broad ideological spectrum, its slow pace in granting full voting rights, and its acceptance of corporate money as a decisive factor in elections, the United States compares unfavorably to most European (and many non-European) nations as a showcase of democracy. Despite reality, however, the idea endured that although American-style democracy might be flawed, no one had ever come up with a better system of government. For most Americans, particularly Democrats, that myth was debunked in 2000.

The big story of 2000 was the Bush v. Gore Florida recount crisis. All manner of malfeasance popped up during five ugly weeks: African-Americans blocked by the police from voting, white right-wing thugs sent to beat up election officials, threats of a military coup by the future president's emissary, systemic political corruption, a ballot-counting system based on approximation, the idiocy of the Electoral College system, and in the end, the blatant corruption of the nation's highest court in choosing one party over the other without bothering to count the votes.

In July 2001, six months after Bush was sworn in, a *USA*

Today/CNN/Gallup poll asked the public whether Bush had won "fair and square." The results were not in his favor: 51 percent said no; 48 percent said yes. Over one quarter—26 percent—of the respondents did not accept Bush as a "legitimate" president. (Bear in mind that coverage of the stolen 2000 election was close to nonexistent at the time the poll was taken, presumably reducing popular outrage.)

But what's important is not the shameful means by which the 2000 election was "won." It is what happened after half the population decided that their new president had cheated his way into the highest elected office in the land: nothing.

Democratic opponent Al Gore believed he had been wronged—yet he was in a hurry to concede. (After initially conceding to Bush on election night, angry advisors persuaded him to retract his concession.) Gore's early passivity set the tone for what ought to have been an active resistance to electoral fraud. In most other democratic countries—hell, in most other undemocratic countries, too—the slightest whiff that a major election has been stolen prompts riots and other civil disturbances, even revolutions. In Kenya, for example, twenty thousand people remain homeless following post-election riots in 2007.

To their credit, professional activist leaders like Reverend Jesse Jackson did threaten street protests in 2000. "We're not planning civil disobedience," said Brian Becker, co-director of the New York–based International Action Center, "but we are planning to fill the streets of Washington with thousands of people" if Bush was declared the winner. However, when the U.S. Supreme Court halted the recount process, effectively declaring Bush the forty-third president, the threats issued by Jackson and other progressives proved empty. There were far fewer than "thousands of people" marching in the streets of Washington to declare their opposition and demand that every vote be counted.

To be precise, the number of protesters was zero. As was the number of protests.

A year after these unseemly nonevents, I appeared on ABC television's *Politically Incorrect* hosted by Bill Maher. One topic of the program was the 9/11 attacks and their political aftermath. When I told the live audience that I thought Bush was using the attacks to retroactively legitimize his presidency, which millions thought he had stolen, Maher slapped me down. "Oh, Ted," he scoffed, "that is so September 10th." The audience laughed.

It *was* funny. Maher is a funny man. And he wrote a nice introduction to one of my books. Still, I was outraged. I remember thinking, the American people have given up on democracy. If we don't care that someone stole the U.S. presidency—remember, this is something that 51 percent of the American people believed—then we are no longer vested in the system. It's dead to us. People might not be able to articulate it in this way, but we're saying we want something new.

9/11: DAY OF THE PAPER TIGER

And so democracy was hanging by a thread when, on September 11, 2001, nineteen hijackers seized four passenger jets and flew three of them into buildings. They killed three thousand people and caused more than twenty billion dollars in insured property damage at the World Trade Center site alone. "America was targeted for attack because we're the brightest beacon for freedom and opportunity in the world," claimed George W. Bush afterward. But the result was less damaging to the concepts of freedom and opportunity than to the aura of military invincibility that the United States seeks to cultivate.

The attacks against the World Trade Center and Pentagon complexes marked a second blow to America's image as an invincible superpower. This time it was the military that was unmasked as a paper tiger, unable to protect its own citizens in its own capital and financial center.

First, the nineteen *jihadis* breached airport security with appalling ease, using primitive weapons that ought to have been intercepted by airport metal detectors. (In addition to the four hijacked planes, the initial conspiracy was apparently broader. Knives and box cutters were found aboard two planes grounded on 9/11. "These look like inside jobs," a government official told *Time* magazine.[30]) Then they operated unimpeded for nearly two full hours in American airspace. And the authorities had known about the hijackings for most of that time. Why should anyone respect or fear a military that couldn't stop such a small-time operation?

This should not have happened in a country that dedicates such a vast share of its resources to military spending. The Pentagon currently accounts for 48 percent of the world's total expenditures on the machinery and infrastructure of offensive and defensive warfare. During 2001 American taxpayers shelled out $1.6 trillion in discretionary military spending, amounting to about 46 percent of the total federal budget. But none of that made a difference when it counted—when the U.S. mainland came under attack for the first time in more than a century.

Where was the U.S. Air Force? Most countries keep fighter jets in the air at all times in order to patrol their airspace. When the attacks began, the number of fighter jets in the air—which could have shot down the planes before they struck their targets—was zero. On the ground, only fourteen jets, all part of the "weekend warrior" Air National Guard, were on standby. These constituted the sum total of military air defense for the contiguous forty-eight states.

You know how action films depict the American military juggernaut as a blend of manic energy and high-technology marvels? September 11 proved that *Top Gun* is only a movie.

At 8:20 a.m. a flight attendant called American Airlines to tell them that flight 11 had been hijacked. It took at least a half hour for the information to be relayed through the airline and military bureaucracies. Personnel were paralyzed by a culture of retribution against workers who speak up and rewards for those who don't. What if it was a false alarm? No one wanted to get in trouble.

Even more amazing than the success of the hijackers in getting control of the planes was the lethargy of the airborne military response. As late as 9:36, according to the 9/11 Commission, "[Federal Aviation Administration] personnel well above [air traffic controllers] in the chain of command had to make the decision to seek military assistance and were working on the issue." An hour later, the Air Force ordered armed F-16s to scramble. An hour! Antiquated radars failed to find the hijacked planes, placed them hundreds of miles away from their actual locations, and reported them as still being in the air after they had crashed. According to *The 9/11 Commission Report*: "The [air traffic control] center tried to contact a former alert site in Atlantic City, unaware it had been phased out." A different squadron was sent to Washington, but no one bothered to tell the pilots about the attacks or why they were being sent there. Without instructions, they flew out over the Atlantic Ocean to conduct routine training exercises.

Though co-opted into silence, some members of the

commission were privately outraged by what they learned about the incompetence of the well-funded U.S. military. "The 10-member commission, in a secret meeting at the end of its tenure in summer 2004, debated referring the matter to the Justice Department for criminal investigation," reported the *Washington Post* in 2006.[31] In a 2007 book about their work for the commission, Thomas Kean and Lee Hamilton accused the Pentagon brass of lying to cover up their idiocy: "If the military had had the amount of time they said they had . . . and had scrambled their jets, it was hard to figure out how they had failed to shoot down at least one of the planes."[32]

Even more than the supposedly "controlled" collapse of the Twin Towers, the government's failure to intercept the hijacked planes gave rise to popular conspiracy theories. If the Air Force had more than enough time to shoot down some or all four planes, why didn't they? Some conspiracy theorists believe that the military had been ordered to "stand down" on 9/11 in order to allow the attacks to occur. "There is only one explanation for this. . . . Our Air Force was ordered to Stand Down on 9/11,"[33] said the webmaster of a 9/11 "truther" site.

The public is divided between those who think the government is evil (because they "let" the attacks occur) and those like me, who think it's run by morons. Whether you believe that the government can't protect us or won't protect us, the myth of a nation that spends a disproportionate percentage of its resources on arms because they're necessary to keep us safe was dealt a fatal blow on 9/11.

The government's commitment to democracy has been exposed as a joke. The public has lost faith in public officials' ability to protect them from foreign threats. Four years later, the federal government would be exposed as incompetent—so inept that it couldn't react to weather.

THE BIG LIE WE ALL ACCEPTED

In March 2003 U.S. forces invaded Iraq. As has been exhaustively documented in shelves of books, the primary pretext given by Bush administration officials for a war that would ultimately kill more than two million people was that Iraq possessed "weapons of mass destruction"—nuclear, biological, and/or chemical weapons proscribed under the ceasefire agreement that ended the 1991 Gulf War.

"Simply stated, there is no doubt that Saddam Hussein now has weapons of mass destruction,"[34] Vice President Dick Cheney told an audience of war veterans in August 2002. "We know for a fact that there are weapons there,"[35] said White House Press Secretary Ari Fleischer in January 2003. "We have sources that tell us that Saddam Hussein recently authorized Iraqi field commanders to use chemical weapons—the very weapons the dictator tells us he does not have,"[36] said George W. Bush in February 2003. Days before the "shock and awe" campaign that devastated

Baghdad, Bush asserted: "Intelligence gathered by this and other governments leaves no doubt that the Iraq regime continues to possess and conceal some of the most lethal weapons ever devised."[37]

Special teams of U.S. soldiers scoured U.S.-occupied Iraq during the spring, summer, and fall of 2003, searching for WMDs. "We'll find them. It'll be a matter of time to do so,"[38] Bush assured the public in May. But then the spin changed.

"We never believed that we'd just tumble over weapons of mass destruction in that country,"[39] said Defense Secretary Donald Rumsfeld in May 2003. "We've only been there seven weeks," he exclaimed on another occasion. "It's a country the size of California—it's not as though we've managed to look *everywhere*."[40]

A few weeks later in the same month, one of the administration's chief neoconservatives and war hawks, Paul Wolfowitz, fessed up to what most Americans were already beginning to suspect: "For bureaucratic reasons, we settled on one issue, weapons of mass destruction (as justification for invading Iraq), because it was the one reason everyone could agree on."[41]

Conning the country to war isn't new. Lyndon B. Johnson did it in 1964, demanding that Congress approve the escalation of the Vietnam conflict to a full-fledged war based on the Tonkin Gulf Incident—the firing of missiles on U.S. Navy vessels—an event that never occurred.

Moreover, the administration argued for deposing Saddam's regime on other grounds, such as democratizing the Middle East and eliminating an existential threat to Israel, a U.S. ally. But WMDs was the big reason, the one that got most of the public (and Congress) behind the effort.

What was new about this war based on lies was the American public's disinterest. The media and the White House held their breath throughout 2003. The longer the long-advertised WMDs failed to turn up, everyone thought, the more anger would build. Surely Bush and his top officials would be impeached or forced to resign. Richard Nixon, who faced impeachment charges for lying to Congress and the American public, was an angel next to these guys.

Yet nothing happened. Again.

Just as the public had collectively shrugged after the stolen election of 2000, not even the hundreds of thousands of people who had marched against the invasion in early 2003 could summon up the outrage required to organize more demonstrations.

This would not have happened a few decades ago.

When a people succumb to apathy, when they fail to police their government because they've learned to expect it to lie to them, when a government learns that it doesn't have to fear the people, one of two things has transpired.

First, the people no longer think that "their" government represents them. They are afraid of it, and/or they view it with contempt.

Or, second, they have lost faith in their ability to affect their own lives. They have become passive. They are broken.

If the second is true, a government may be pleased that its people are broken. But they should be scared.

People don't stay broken forever.

A SURPRISE THAT WASN'T

In 2005 the long-predicted "direct hit" on New Orleans materialized in the form of Hurricane Katrina, which devastated the city as well as much of the Gulf Coast of the southeastern United States. Once again, a noxious brew of stupidity and carelessness turned a potentially manageable threat into a disaster. At least eighteen hundred people died; initial damage assessments ranged upward of one hundred billion dollars. Systemic racism, poverty, and the government's attendant long-term neglect of infrastructure endemic to the region transformed a disaster into a catastrophe with long-term consequences—including the loss of the American people's faith in their government's willingness and ability to respond to . . . bad weather.

At this writing, thousands of displaced residents of Mississippi and Louisiana are living in ramshackle trailers, reduced to the status of internal refugees. More than one million people were permanently displaced by the hurricane and its aftermath—which included a descent into looting, anarchy, and economic collapse—turning it into the largest diaspora in American history, eclipsing the Dust Bowl and Civil War.[42]

As on 9/11, nonresponsiveness was the order of the day. Days after the hurricane had left the city of New Orleans, television crews captured scenes of mayhem as residents looted stores in search of food and water. They were not criminals—they were hungry and thirsty people with nowhere else to turn for supplies. Helicopters flew over people holding signs—"help," "please send food"—while waiting out the floods on the roofs of their homes. When the government finally arrived in force, it wasn't to help. It was to establish "command and control" over the population.

Forty-six thousand National Guardsmen descended on the city, unleashing an orgy of state violence on the needy and desperate. "They have M16s and are locked and loaded. These troops know how to shoot and kill and I expect they will,"[43] said Louisiana Governor Kathleen Blanco. They did. At least eight of residents were shot to death by New Orleans police officers who casually picked off pedestrians as they drove through town. The officers did not provide food or water.[44]

Even now, years later, it's hard to tell why the government stood by and let the city of New Orleans be destroyed, dispatching troops rather than help. This "command and control" policy hasn't changed since Barack Obama took office; its deployment during the 2010 earthquake in Haiti caused thousands of people to die needlessly.[45]

In New Orleans, meanwhile, both the city's economy and population appear to have been permanently hobbled. If Bush's top officials thought the rest of the country would perceive New Orleans as a "black city" that could easily be ignored, they were mistaken. Perhaps because so many had visited as tourists, the death of New Orleans and the government's response—stinking slabs of ineptitude and neglect wrapped in a rotten burrito of violence—shocked citizens of all races and classes. If it could happen to "them"—the blacks of New Orleans—it could happen to anyone.

Post-Katrina, a *Newsweek* poll from September 2005 found that Bush's popularity had plummeted to 38 percent, down from a post-9/11 high of 91 percent. "But Katrina's most costly impact could be a loss of faith in government generally," reported the magazine.

Gee, ya think?

Fifty-seven percent of respondents to the poll said the "government's slow response to what happened in New Orleans" made them "lose confidence in government's ability to deal with another major natural disaster. . . . Forty-seven percent say it has made them lose confidence in the government's ability to prevent another terrorist attack like 9/11."[46]

Politicians recognized the threat to their legitimacy. They tried to counteract it from inside the system, deploying a classic strategy: isolate some entity or person, scapegoat it, and then replace, reform, or get rid of it. They

122 The Anti-American Manifesto

went after the Federal Emergency Management Agency (FEMA) and its hapless leader, Michael Brown. "FEMA has become a symbol of bumbling bureaucracy in which the American people have completely lost faith,"[47] said Susan Collins, the Republican chairwoman of the Senate Homeland Security and Governmental Affairs Committee a year later. She announced the formation of a new agency, the National Preparedness and Response Authority, which would have, had it ever been created, reported directly to the president during disasters.

But it was too late to reverse the damage to the government's credibility. Having witnessed the death-by-neglect of New Orleans, Americans don't expect their government to help when the chips are down.

This is worse for the government than for the people.

OBAMA FAILS THE TEST: THE FINAL CRISIS OF AMERICAN CAPITALISM

The fifth crisis of the Bush era became the first crisis faced by Obama. Even without the first three, it was and remains a more serious threat to the current political order than the first four combined. A shaky economy built on easy credit, increasing wage disparity, and speculation finally came crashing down.

According to government agencies, the economies of first world nations are either beginning the fourth year of a severe recession—one whose existence they denied until autumn 2008—or are at the beginning of a tenuous, long (jobless) recovery. As anyone who looks for work knows, however, the "Great Recession"—in truth, a depression—began in 2001. That's when the dot-com crash metastasized into a decline in consumer spending and squeezed credit. Remember, the first seven years of the Bush presidency were no picnic for American workers. They were characterized by growing deficits, shrinking tax receipts, net job losses (when allowing for population growth in the work force), and wage stagnation.

The economic collapse that began in September 2008 exposed not only the inherent shortcomings of the U.S. variant of liberal capitalism, but also the corporate-political ruling class's inability to figure out what—to paraphrase Freud—men and women in the United States want. At this writing, the answer is simple and obvious: jobs. While the official unemployment rate exceeds 10 percent, the "real" jobless rate—the number of American workers who want work but have run out of unemployment benefits, are substantially underemployed by number of hours and/or skills, and/or have accepted reality and given up looking for work, which is how the rate was calculated until the 1970s—exceeds 20 percent. (During the deepest trough of the Great Depression, unemployment peaked at 25 percent, but exceeded 20 percent only between 1933 and 1935.)

Americans need jobs. But the U.S. government has forgotten how to create them.

During the Great Depression, socialism and the populist anger channeled by figures such as Louisiana governor Huey Long led to a real crisis of capitalism. President Franklin Roosevelt's New Deal softened the blow, "saving capitalism from itself," in the historians' vernacular, pumping federal money into the economy and vesting citizens by directly employing more than eight million workers to build public infrastructure and other projects. But just because people *want* jobs doesn't mean that they're going get them.

The current global financial crisis has a lot in common with the Great Depression sparked by the 1929 Wall Street crash: it was caused by a real estate bubble that fueled speculation in securities and precipitated bank failures. This led to a loss of confidence that, in turn, caused credit markets to seize up. Auto manufacturers declared bankruptcy and requested bailouts from the federal government. Oil and food prices hit record highs as unemployment soared.

The federal government's initial response was the same in both cases: both the Hoover and Bush administrations bailed out the largest failing banks in the hope that they would loosen credit again. Hoover, a former businessman who maintained close ties to his old Wall Street colleagues, hoped that his bailouts would increase liquidity and inspire banks to begin issuing new loans again. But the

bankers balked. The underlying weakness of the con-
sumer-based economy couldn't justify new lending. Too
many people were unemployed and underemployed, too
few businesses enjoyed bright prospects. It didn't work in
1930 and it didn't work in 2008. Banks shored up their
balance sheets with taxpayer money; they knew better than
to lend to borrowers who could no longer look forward to
constant paper increases in home values to serve as col-
lateral. Unemployment soared. So did foreclosures. Tent
cities appeared.

In 1932, however, voters rejected the top-down proto-
trickle-down approach favored by the Republicans in favor
of FDR's "build from the bottom up" direct-employment
programs. Employment rose—until 1937, when deficit
hawks persuaded the president to curtail public works programs in favor of paying down the rising national debt.
Ultimately, the full employment program called World War
II ended the Great Depression.

Roosevelt's approach might have worked in 2009.
Instead, Obama followed the path laid out by Hoover:
shoveling trillions of federal tax dollars into the coffers of
banks, insurance companies, and large automobile manufacturers. Obama's men were and are so vested in, so
owned by, so terrified of their corporate masters that they
could not act to save capitalism from itself. They could only
watch passively as unemployment continued to rise, further undermining their own claim to rule.

As the un- and underemployment rate climbed, Obama pointed instead to a "green economy"—let a thousand solar panels bloom!—as the Internet of the twenty-first century, the magical economic transformation that would bring about recovery, as the development of the World Wide Web did during the 1990s. Alan Salzman, CEO of VantagePoint Venture Partners, which has invested billions in green industries, claimed: "Cleantech is going to be the industrial revolution of the 21st century."[48]

Obama sang the same tune. "Building a robust clean energy sector is how we will create the jobs of the future, jobs that pay well and can't be outsourced," claimed the beleaguered president, his approval ratings falling faster than any other U.S. leader in the history of polling. But even the most optimistic assessments of the possible, maybe, you-never-know "green jobs revolution" are unimpressive. "One report by the Rand Corporation and University of Tennessee found that if 25 percent of all American energy were produced from renewable sources by 2025, we would generate at least five million new green jobs," reported *Time* magazine in 2008.

With official unemployment over seventeen million and the real rate double that, green jobs won't save the U.S. economy. Workers can't wait until 2025. As lame as the Rand projection was, Obama's actions paled in comparison: "Obama announced $2.3 billion in tax credits—to be paid for from last year's $787 stimulus package—that he said would create some seventeen thousand 'green' jobs," reported the Associated Press on January 8, 2010."The money will go to projects including solar, wind and energy management."[49]

The U.S. economy needs to add one hundred thousand new jobs a month to keep up with population growth and keep the unemployment rate even. At this writing, in March 2010, it would require four hundred thousand new jobs each month for three years to get back to December 2007.

Seventeen thousand jobs? Was Obama still using drugs?

From the standpoint of American progressives and liberals, Barack Obama has been either a disappointment or a disaster. But his failures also present us with a unique opportunity to remake our country and solve the pressing problems facing us today.

Obama has delivered small-bore improvements to his left-of-center political base: a heartfelt but halfhearted attempt to tweak the healthcare and financial services industries, kicking banks out of the college student loan business, adding land to the protection of the national parks service, giving representatives of organized labor a seat at the table, increasing the minimum wage, and extending unemployment benefits.

Obviously, these improvements would not have occurred under Republican rule. At the same time, Obama has deployed a Clintonian "triangulation" strategy (taking the "middle ground" between and "above" the left and the right) which has resulted in policies that the Republican right was unable to achieve, such as Obama's 2010 decision to eliminate a long-standing ban on offshore oil drilling.

On the big issues of war, peace, and the economy, moreover, Obama has been even worse for liberals than George W. Bush. Obama's signature achievement to date, his healthcare initiative, contained no "public option" provision, promises to increase Americans' overall spending on health insurance, and was crafted primarily to protect insurance company profits.

Obama has continued Bush's disastrous military occupations of Afghanistan and Iraq, his domestic spying program, the right to torture and hold detainees indefinitely, the extraordinary rendition program, and his top-down economic policy. Unlike Bush, however, Obama is supposedly a Democrat. He is the first African-American president. He put a smart, likeable face on policies most people found reprehensible under his predecessor. And so liberals have been reluctant to criticize him. Liberal legislators within his party and activists on the outside have sat on their hands. Bush-era protest signs have been packed away.

**Americans live shorter lives than citizens of almost every other
developed country, ranking forty-second in terms of life
expectancy. This is down from eleventh two decades ago.**
—Associated Press[50]

Obama is Bush minus opposition.

"The illegal wars and occupations, the largest transference
of wealth upward in American history and the egregious
assault on civil liberties, all begun under George W. Bush,
raise only a flicker of tepid protest from liberals when prop-
agated by the Democrats," the journalist Chris Hedges
complained in early 2010. "The timidity of the Left exposes its
cowardice, lack of a moral compass and mounting political
impotence. The Left stands for nothing."[51]

Therein lies the opportunity. Hedges's solution—supporting the Green Party and other third parties—is
bullshit. No one thinks that will work. Revolution will.
What matters is that Obama has exposed the two-party
system for what it has always been: ineffective, disconnected, and removed from the people. Populist rhetoric
aside, both parties serve the rich. Now everyone can see
that. The next step is to convince people that the answer
isn't new parties, but a different political system.

Young people, minorities, and working-class people
energized by Obama's campaign in 2008 have become so
disgusted that many of them will never again involve

themselves in the official political process. Clinton labor secretary Robert Reich calls it "the enthusiasm gap": "The Dem base is lethargic because congressional Democrats continue to compromise on everything the Dem base cares about. For a year now it's been nothing but compromises, watered-down ideas, weakened provisions, wider loopholes, softened regulations."[52]

Under the existing system, apathy is one logical course of (in)action for a thinking person. Once presented with the possibility of throwing out the old system and building a new one, however, radicalization can replace apathy.

"Anyone with an ounce of sanity," continues Reich, "understands government is the only effective countervailing force against the forces that got us into this mess." True. But not this government. Not this president. Reich concedes as much, blaming "the rot at the center of the system" on "big business's and Wall Street's generous flows of campaign donations to Dems, coupled with their implicit promise of high-paying jobs once Democratic officials retire from government."[53]

They won't reform their cozy system voluntarily.

TAPPED OUT . . . AND TAPPING INTO ANGER

Obama can't fix the economy. And it can't fix itself. Consumers would need to start spending. That won't happen for three reasons.

First, workers whose wages have stagnated or declined in real terms for the last four decades can no longer keep up with the rising costs of housing, healthcare, higher education, and food, which, in spite of official figures indicating inflation in the low single digits, have actually been running above 5 percent for most of the last ten years. (The website Shadow Government Statistics provides figures consistent with the methodology used to calculate inflation prior to 1993.[54])

Second, those forty years of declining real wages and tax policies designed to discourage deposits to savings accounts means people don't have savings. In 2005, before the start of the fiscal crisis, the national savings rate hit zero for the first time since the Great Depression. The average American family had a pitiful one thousand dollars in savings.

Finally, credit, the consumer's tool of last resort, has failed. Like an engine deprived of fuel, the economy is stalled. The Obamaites could jumpstart it—but they won't because they're slaves to short-term moneyed interests.

Meanwhile, while taxpayers can least afford it, cash-strapped states and municipalities are increasing income, sales, and property taxes. At the same time, the feds are joining municipalities at cutting back services. At this writing, the Postal Service is considering abolishing Saturday mail delivery. All over the country, mass transit systems are getting rid of bus and train service at

night, on weekends, and holidays. Pay more, get less—
is there a more efficient formula for fostering anger and
resentment?

As people's lives get worse, annoyance will devolve into
anger. Then rage. Any spark will set it off—and a spark will
come. The question for us is, will we channel populist anger
into productive, positive, radical, revolutionary change?

One of our best allies is the governmental-corporate
propaganda machine. Media manipulators understand
that the mass delusion economists call consumer confidence is fragile. Despite corporate employers' exploitation
of economic contractions in order to exert downward pressure on wages, even they know that "talking down the
economy" too long could kill the goose that lays two-thirds
of economic activity: consumerism. For this reason, recessions that last years are said "officially" to last only a little
over a year. The post-Reagan bust that began in 1987, for
example, was not formally acknowledged by mainstream
economists and media to have begun until 1990.
According to them, recovery began in 1991. In truth, 1991
was a terrible year. I remember because it was the year I
graduated from college. For the first time in memory,
Columbia University canceled its annual job fair because
not one single prospective employer was interested in
attending. If you were looking for work, the job market
remained tight through 1994.

The media can talk about recovery all they want. In the

real world, there are only two reliable indicators of economic strength: employment and wages. To say that an economic recovery is underway during a period of high unemployment is as nonsensical as saying that it's a sunny day except for all that rain. If you're part of the elite, however, you might not care about those two things, but only about how much profit you and your fellow ruling-class members can accumulate (which is why they can say the economy is good while most people are struggling).

True to form, the state-sanctioned media has already declared the beginning of a recovery. (Sometimes they call it a "jobless recovery." Sorry. No such thing.) In November 2009, Mark Zandi, a chief economist at Moody's, became the first to declare (in the *New York Times*) that "the Great Recession is over. The solid 3.5 percent gain in gross domestic product during the third quarter [of 2009] proves that the longest, broadest and most severe American downturn since the 1930s has finally given way to recovery." Granted, Zandi allowed, "Businesses may not be shedding jobs as aggressively as they were earlier this year, but they still aren't hiring." Could it be that there aren't many jobs left to shed? Or that declaring a recovery based on a single quarterly increase in GDP is nonsense? Even as job losses continue to pile up, numerous mainstream economists have since gone on record to argue that a recovery is underway.

Or could it be that these terms are defined by people who have a completely different set of standards about what life should be like? If wealth is still flowing upward, even at our expense, they consider it a good day.

For the first time in years, the Department of Labor's Bureau of Statistics announced a net increase in jobs for the month of March 2010. One hundred sixty-two thousand jobs had been created. After subtracting the net gain in jobs needed to keep up with population growth, that left sixty-two thousand jobs created—a few molecules in a drop in the U.S. economy.

Then the downward trend resumed.

How many people are out of work? No one knows for sure. For example, forty-eight million Americans are stay-at-home parents. Many of them would work if they could—but they don't count as unemployed. Ask anyone who works in retail, however, and they will paint a grim picture: empty stores, empty cash registers.

No one on Main Street believes the squawkers of Wall Street. But media propagandists serve a revolutionary purpose. As the powers that be attempt to talk up the economy in the op-ed pages of newspapers that are themselves teetering on the brink of bankruptcy, they alienate the millions of people who are out of work or underemployed. Watching news reports of an economy that seems to boom without them is maddening. The system's propaganda machine can't help repeating its message that everything is going to be fine, that its actions have prevented things from getting even worse. This stream of propaganda disconnects the government from the people whose consent it requires to remain in power. Every new insult to the people's intelligence provides another powerful wedge for revolutionary forces to exploit.

Added to the combustible mix of increasing poverty and governmental insensitivity is the broad sense that things are not going to get better. Help is not on the way. The cavalry is not coming.

15.8 percent of Americans, or 47.4 million people, live in poverty.
—Associated Press[55]

Unlike the recession that cost George H. W. Bush reelection in 1992, there's no dot-com boom or other technological breakthrough waiting in the wings to create new demand. Moreover, globalization has increased economic interconnectivity to the extent that there isn't a new set of deep-pocketed foreign investors (the Japanese of the 1980s, the Chinese of the 1990s) to buy U.S. government debt or invest in private companies. And the federal government can't do what's necessary to save itself—nationalize banks and major industries, directly employ tens of millions of workers, forgive home mortgages and credit card debts—

without offending its corporate masters (who are too stupid and short-sighted to understand that those steps would save them, too).

If every system contains the seeds of its future demise, American capitalism's tendency to concentrate wealth in fewer and fewer hands at an ever-accelerating pace since the Vietnam War has led it to the brink of an epochal crisis that is most certainly "the worst since the Great Depression." In truth, it could be *worse* than the Great Depression before it's over. The nation hasn't lost intrinsic wealth. Too few simply have too much. So money, the lifeblood of the economy, has stopped circulating. American capitalism was structurally unsound from the beginning. Now it is plainly dead.

THE JOYS OF DOWNWARD MOBILITY

Even if Obama's plan had worked as advertised, it would have been too little, too late. At best, his advisors predict that their modest stimulus will create four million new jobs in a couple of years. But that's a drop in the bucket next to the eleven-plus million jobs lost since the depression began in 2008—a figure currently projected to increase by at least one or two million each year.

Homelessness and hunger, even to the point of starvation, could soon become widespread problems for millions of Americans who had formerly counted themselves among the middle class.

Jobless people are scared, desperate, and angry, especially when their spouses and family members have also lost jobs. And with an estimated six people applying for every available opening, those who still do have jobs are worried that they'll be next, and that the dismal employment climate will weaken their negotiations with management for decent salaries and working conditions. These fears are warranted: hours have been cut, wages have been frozen, and furloughs are commonplace. Crime, on the wane until 2008, is rising. People are turning mean. "Although there are no hard data connecting violence with economic downturns, periods of economic difficulty have been linked to increases in violent behavior," reported the *Christian Science Monitor* in early 2010. "For instance, a study released last March by the Florida Department of Children and Families revealed that the state saw an almost forty percent increase in demand for domestic-violence centers, which it said was related to the poor economy."[56]

In the United States, a murder is committed every thirty-one minutes, one rape every 5.8 minutes, and one burglary every 14.5 seconds.
—*Washington Post*, September 16, 2008[57]

During the first year of the fiscal collapse, there were many cases of fired workers committing suicide, sometimes after murdering former coworkers or members of their family. On November 14, 2008, in Santa Clara, California, Jing Hua Wu, forty-seven, shot three people to death with a nine-millimeter handgun inside the technology company office where he had just been fired. One of the people he shot was the CEO. In Brockport, New York, on Valentine's Day 2009 Frank Garcia, thirty-five, opened fire in the parking lot of a hospital that had just canned him. He shot three people there, killing two former coworkers, then shot a married couple execution-style inside their home. On January 7, 2010, fifty-one-year-old Timothy Hendron entered a St. Louis transformer manufacturing facility with an assault rifle, shotgun, and pistol; he had sued the company for ripping off his 401(k) retirement plan. He shot three coworkers before placing the gun under his chin and blowing himself away. Five days later, in Kennesaw, Georgia, a disgruntled ex-employee stormed a truck rental business in camouflage and opened fire with a handgun, killing two people and critically wounding three others. On February 10, 2010, a Harvard-educated neurologist got into the act. After being denied tenure, Professor Amy Bishop shot six of her colleagues, killing three.

Anger isn't limited to the unemployed. The 2010 Conference Board survey of American workers found a record high rate of dissatisfaction among those who managed to hold on to their jobs.

"It is not about the business cycle or one grumpy generation," says Linda Barrington, managing director of human capital at the Conference Board, but rather the culmination of a two-decades-old trend. Jobs are less interesting, more stressful, less well paid, and feature fewer benefits than in the past. So unhappy with their jobs are American workers, adds Lynn Franco, director of the consumer research center at the Conference Board, that they prefer sitting in traffic to sitting at their desks: "The commute to work ranks number one as the most satisfying aspect of one's job."[58]

Anger has turned political. On February 18, 2010, Joe Stack flew his small plane into an IRS office in Austin, Texas, killing one worker. Before his suicide attack, the "self-radicalized" terrorist published his complaints about the government online. "Why is it that a handful of thugs and plunderers can commit unthinkable atrocities (and in the case of the GM executives, for scores of years) and when it's time for their gravy train to crash under the weight of their gluttony and overwhelming stupidity, the force of the full federal government has no difficulty coming to their aid within days if not hours?" Stack wrote. "Yet at the same time, the joke we call the American medical system, including the drug and insurance companies, are murdering tens of thousands of people a year and stealing from the corpses and victims they cripple, and this country's leaders don't see this as important as bailing out a few of their vile, rich cronies."[59] Two weeks later, John

Bedell, thirty-six, walked into the Pentagon and shot two guards. He, too, had posted his political complaints on the Internet: "The moral values of individuals and communities are increasingly attacked by a political system where deceit is routine and accepted and the only standard is power,"[60] Bedell asserted.

Social and political instability will push the safety net provided by federal and local authorities, already stretched to its limits due to shrinking tax bases and lack of foresight during better times, past its breaking point. It is not inconceivable that regions of the nation such as New York and New England, which send more federal tax dollars to Washington than they get back, will see revived secessionist movements, egged on by opportunistic (and perhaps desperate) local political figures.

It has often been remarked by defenders of American-style liberal capitalism that poor Americans live better than the middle classes do in many other countries. They are right. Most have televisions and other electronic appliances. Not only is starvation not a problem, they suffer from obesity. If the people aren't hungry enough, the saying goes, they won't revolt. That goes threefold for America's self-defined "middle class." Fifty-three percent of Americans define themselves as middle class, including 40 percent of those earning less than twenty thousand dollars a year and a third of those earning more than one hundred fifty thousand!

But they may feel plenty hungry soon enough. A sizeable share of these self-defined middle-class success stories will lose their jobs and therefore their homes. Eviction notices will spread. Electricity will get cut off. More cars will be repossessed. And their government, especially their federal government, will be either unwilling or unable to help.

There will be anger. More and more anger.

OBAMA'S KATRINA: THE BP OIL SPILL IN THE GULF

The April 20, 2010, explosion that destroyed British Petroleum's Deepwater Horizon oil drilling platform in the Gulf of Mexico, killing eighteen workers and decimating one of the nation's major tourist destinations, ended Barack's Obama's honeymoon with the media and, more importantly, with many of his supporters. It marked the death of the President's "hopey changey" (Sarah Palin's insipidly dismissive yet prescient description of Obama's 2008 sales pitch) persona. And it placed in yet sharper relief what became clear from the four major crises that shattered Americans' faith in government during the Bush years: the system is bankrupt, our leaders are corrupt, and the people can count only upon ourselves.

As I write this in July of 2010, crude oil has been pouring into the Gulf of Mexico for three months. Efforts to stop the flow have been stymied by the extreme cold and high pressure at the site of the blowout some five thousand feet below sea level. Both BP and federal authorities claim that America's worst oil spill in history is now under control. Even if the attempt to plug the leak holds, however, the full consequences of the disaster will not be known for years.

As any editor will tell you, the best stories—those with legs—are those with a "drip, drip, drip" quality. Setting aside the anti-Muslim bigotry that mitigated some Americans' response to the photos of torture by America soldiers of Iraqi prisoners at Abu Ghraib, one reason that people didn't demand accountability was that the story didn't continue. The photos were released. We saw them. That was it. Had the same images been released over time—ideally, beginning with the least awful and slowly building up to the truly disgusting—the impact and thus the consequences would probably have been far greater.

By definition the BP spill in the Gulf has had everything an editor or television news producer could ask for: a catastrophe getting worse by the day (nay, the second!); beautiful beaches blackened by gunk; pelicans, dolphins, and other telegenic creatures choking and dying because corporate executives cheaped out on equipment that might have prevented the disaster in the first place. Every night on the evening news, it was more of the same horror.

One month into the crisis, people asked: Where is the

government? Where is Obama? Why haven't federal agencies taken over the effort to plug the Deepwater Horizon well? Why was BP allowed to (a) drill so deep and (b) drill so deep without adequate safety measures?

The anger has grown.

Still, Obama's team doesn't get it. Even after newspapers published accounts that described an oil industry that had corrupted the agencies that were supposed to regulate it, the Department of the Interior continued to issue permits for new offshore drilling. Obama didn't order a halt to new underwater oil rigs for five weeks.

The Gulf filled with oil. Fishermen are going out of business. Beaches have been closed. To add apocalypse to disaster, the same area devastated by Katrina has once again been staring into the abyss. Once again, the government hasn't helped.

And still more oil.

"You're talking about a reservoir that could have tens of millions of barrels in it," David Rensink, incoming president of the American Association of Petroleum Geologists, told National Geographic.

"We don't have any idea how to stop this," said Matthew Simmons, retired chair of the energy-industry investment banking firm Simmons & Company International. Ideas like jamming the leaking pipe with golf balls and other debris are a "joke," he added.

A Purdue engineering professor called before Congress

estimated the flow rate at 95,000 barrels, or 4 million gallons, of crude oil a day—20 times the company's official claim. By July, when a "relief well" was attempted just before the start of hurricane season, the BP spill was already the worst oil disaster ever. The previous record had been set by Iraq in 1991, which dumped 336 million gallons into the Persian Gulf in order to slow down U.S. invasion forces during the Gulf War. Twelve years later, almost all of the Saudi coastline, including its marshes and mudflats, was devoid of life. Contrary to the common belief that spilled crude rises to the surface, meters-thick sediment still coats the floor of the Persian Gulf. Deprived of oxygen, the water above the disaster site is dead. So are the wetlands.

"It was amazing to stand there and look across what used to be a [Saudi] salt marsh and it was all dead—not even a live crab," Miles Hayes, co-founder of the consulting firm Research Planning, Inc. and one of those who studied the 1991 spill's aftermath, recalled.

Lovely.

One could hardly blame BP alone. It's an oil company. Their sole motivation is profits. If they could extract oil from the crushed skulls of newborn babies, they would. Liberal or conservative, people count on government to protect them from corporations run amok. The Gulf spill proved that the U.S. government—even one led by the first black president, a supposedly liberal Democrat—serves Big Oil.

Talk about lousy political timing! Drill, baby, drill, Obama had urged America less than a month before the Deepwater Horizon sunk. "Ultimately, we need to move beyond the tired debates of the left and the right, between business leaders and environmentalists, between those who would claim drilling is a cure all and those who would claim it has no place," the President said on March 31, 2010. Obama gambled and lost big, doomed forever to be remembered as a man who was on the wrong side of history.

"I hold Obama responsible for not making BP stand up and look at the people in the face and fix it," Dean Blanchard, owner of a seafood business, told a protest rally in New Orleans on May 30, 2010, according to Reuters.

But Obama couldn't fix it. Only BP had the equipment and technological knowledge to address the situation. Theoretically, Obama could have seized BP's North American operations through nationalization; it wouldn't have stopped the leak but fishermen and other victims could have received economic compensation. In reality, of course, Obama could no more take on BP than a mouse could eat a cat. He is beholden to big business, both afraid of it and in love with it. It's a sick relationship. More and more Americans are beginning to understand that, as long as it continues, they will suffer.

Except for the millions of dead fish and birds, the ruined livelihoods and environmental devastation, the spill was an event that could help lead us in the right direction. Just as polls indicated that a majority of Americans had begun to doubt that global climate change was happening or was a problem even if it *was* happening, the spill showcased the importance of the environment. It also became an opportunity for those of us who see a better way to live, in harmony with the other living things with which we share the Earth, to make our case. People do care about the planet. That became clear when the Congressional website hosting a livecam positioned at the site of the deepwater gusher crashed—because so many people were trying to watch it at the same time.

"At some point—the widespread debut of the BP 'spillcam' is as good a delineation point as any—this tipped, in the national conversation, from a destructive event into a calamitous, open-ended saga. And for the bruised and cantankerous American psyche, it could not come at a worse time," wrote Ted Anthony and Mary Foster for the Associated Press. "Fear is afoot everywhere, and polarization prevails. Faith in institutions—corporations, government, the media—is down. Americans are angry, and they long ago grew accustomed to expecting the resolution of problems in very short order, even if reality rarely works that way."[61]

The solution to problems like the BP spill is to avoid them in the first place. Drilling a mile under the ocean should never have been permitted, and a decent government would never have allowed it. Drilling for oil in the ocean shouldn't occur either. Putting corporate profits ahead of everyone and everything else—the way America has done things for longer than anyone can remember—suddenly look as stupid and evil as it has been all along.

PISSED OFF AND WIDE AWAKE

The most important thing an American citizen can do today is realize that there is another way to live, that there are, in fact, an infinite number of other ways of life, governmental and economic systems that we should consider emulating, and brand-new ones no one has ever thought of before, waiting to be discovered. But understanding that we are not stuck with this system, indeed that this system can't last even if we want to keep it, isn't nearly enough. We must all take an active role in dismantling the old system and creating the next one.

Unemployment and job insecurity are the Obama administration's and the United States government's biggest weaknesses. They are also would-be revolutionaries' greatest opportunities.

Millions and millions of Americans would choose socialism, communism, libertarianism, anarchism, or other ideological doctrines over what we have now if they believed it would get them their jobs and houses back. Unfettered corporate capitalism partnered with a compliant two-party representative democracy isn't working for the American people. They're finding that out now.

Here is one reason I believe that: in April 2009 a Rasmussen poll found that only 53 percent of Americans thought that capitalism was better than socialism.[62] (Twenty percent prefer socialism; 27 percent didn't know. Asked to be more specific, 15 percent say they support a Soviet-style state-controlled economy wherein the government owns and runs large business concerns.) "Adults under 30 are essentially evenly divided: 37 percent prefer capitalism, 33 socialism, and 30 percent are undecided. Thirty-somethings are a bit more supportive of the free-enterprise approach with 49 percent for capitalism and 26 for socialism."[63] Remember, this is in a nation where "commie" is an epithet and public intellectuals who clearly sympathize with socialism—Noam Chomsky, Ralph Nader, Howard Zinn—are cautious to identify themselves as such.

Whether socialism or some other form of government will follow the end of the current regime is a speculative question. It doesn't matter yet. What matters now is that anywhere between 20 and 47 percent of the American people—and between 30 and 63 percent of the under-forty set who are more likely to take to the streets (or cheer when others do) when the crunch finally comes—have given up on capitalism or are at least willing to entertain a different form of economic organization.

This is huge. Bear in mind, the poll was taken only six months into the global economic meltdown. As more and more people lose their jobs and houses and savings accounts, those figures will likely increase. People already know there are alternatives to careless capitalism. They will start to see them as viable, start to be curious, start to find out more about them.

Those of us who are already radicalized must help others see that change is possible and that real change can only be enacted by us and them together.

About that "real change": can it be effected peacefully, from within the system? Civics teachers and opinion columns suggest yes. History screams no.

THE BIGGEST LIE: CHANGE FROM WITHIN

All ideas, all ideologies, all nations, the idea of nationhood itself—all are tenuous constructs of emotion and faith. Every day, tens of millions of Americans go to work, expecting to be paid in pieces of black and green paper, which they use to buy goods and services. What else is that, but a system of blind faith? Faith that on payday your employer will make good on his promise to pay you, that shops and other suppliers will accept printed paper currency, and that your government will stand behind its currency at full value. Faith doesn't last forever. That the internal inconsistencies that define our country's form of government and its economy be exposed is inevitable. It has always been obvious, for instance, that an economy driven by consumerism (whether or not it's true, the old canard stands that consumers account for two-thirds of economic activity) is unsustainable.

Productivity cannot continue to rise by leaps and bounds; at some point, it has to plateau. Investors who counted on annual returns much higher than the rate of inflation were playing a Ponzi scheme, and they knew it. In the media business, for example, the head of the Knight-Ridder newspaper chain famously guaranteed shareholders a 15 to 20 percent annual increase in share value—this during a period of shrinking circulation and an official inflation rate under 5 percent. His papers were indeed profitable—but profitable wasn't enough. Disappointed investors and bad acquisitions decisions ultimately put Knight-Ridder out of business . . . even though they never lost a penny.

Reform from within is possible—but not the sweeping, radical solutions required to solve fundamental problems. But incremental reform is never likely to occur, much less be effective. Politicians and CEOs are slow to react, unimaginative, and unwilling to reduce their privileges and prerogatives unless they are absolutely forced to do so. Which isn't likely under the present circumstances.

It takes radicals to lead bold fundamental reform. The two major political parties make it their business to push real radicals out of their "big tents." Which out-of-the-box thinker is going to work his way up the political food chain to lead a major party? Dennis Kucinich? Ron Paul? Ralph Nader?

Vladimir Lenin asked, What is to be done? That is always the big political question. Where do we go from here? How do we address our challenges? How can we rise above immediate problems to dream, to work toward making our lives and those of future generations not just as good as we think they ought to be, but as great as we can imagine?

Our priority must be the well-being of the broad majority of the people without ignoring the needs and desires of the many minorities. Well, let's ignore the piggish desires of one minority, the tiny clique of insanely wealthy people and businesses who have all but destroyed our magnificent land and nation. Any form of government that doesn't include improving as many lives as possible doesn't deserve anyone's support. (Yes, including the rich minority. While wealth may be acquired in a society devoid of political stability, it cannot be retained. This is why nineteenth-century robber barons invented philanthropy. Keep the masses happy enough to shut up, and let the cash keep pouring in.)

In this place, at this time (and, I fear, in future times as well), the United States government stands in the way of the American people in its attempt to answer Lenin's question. We may not agree on what needs to be done to ensure better lives and to create more jobs and economic security both within and outside the workplace. As things stand, however, with the U.S. government running interference for corporate interests, there is no point even discussing what to do. Even if our three hundred million people were to arrive at an instantaneous national consensus concerning what to do about jobs, the economy, or any other pressing matter, we could not carry it out.

The U.S. system has had countless chances to prove the efficacy of internal reform. For the past half century, the American political system has faced numerous challenges: income inequality; soaring prices for housing, education, and healthcare; systemic racism. It has come up short.

The United States has the most unequal distribution of income and wages of any high-income country in the last thirty years.
—*New York Times*[64]

The last major social programs enacted by Congress were signed into law by Lyndon Johnson in the mid-1960s. The last major public works built in the U.S. was the federal interstate highway system, mostly completed in the 1950s. A century ago, workers fought for the twelve-hour day, then the ten-hour day, then the eight-hour day. Concomitantly, since the 1950s, as the economist Juliet Schor has documented, workplace productivity has more than doubled. Logically, the four-hour day should now be the norm. But, for those who still have jobs, working hours have risen (to about forty-eight weekly). All the productivity improvements went into executive pay, corporate profits, and stock dividends. Meanwhile, average and median wages stagnated and then began falling.

In late 2009 McGill University physician and researcher Jody Heymann was interviewed by National Public Radio about her new book, the awkwardly titled *Raising the Global Floor: Dismantling the Myth That We Can't Afford Good Working Conditions for Everyone.* Dr. Heymann repeated a grim litany with which we Americans are all too familiar: despite living in the wealthiest country on earth, our social benefits—particularly our working conditions—rank among the worst. On one quality of life issue after another, she and other researchers determined, American workers toiled under conditions that were similar to those of employees in third world countries like Myanmar, Papua New Guinea, Sierra Leone, and Lesotho. (These last two had recently experienced civil wars.) More than one hundred other countries, including all of the industrialized nations, do better by their people on the number of paid sick days employers are required to provide, paid and unpaid maternity and paternity days (Mexico provides six months paid maternity leave both before and after a birth), personal days for moves and caring for sick relatives, and so on. One hundred fifty-seven nations don't even *allow* you to work for more than six days in a row—you have to take the seventh day off. Like God.

This was a call-in show. Caller after caller asked Dr. Heymann why the U.S. fared so poorly compared to the rest of the world, especially since both wealthy and poor nations were happy to provide these benefits to their workers. She repeatedly ducked the question, reiterating the facts. One hundred sixty-four nations guarantee paid vacation days in their labor laws; the U.S. does not. One hundred sixty-three nations guarantee paid sick days; the U.S. does not.

YOU CAN FIGHT CITY HALL, BUT YOU CAN'T WIN

Finally the host, Diane Rehm, brought up the U word: unions. Could it be, Rehm (no liberal, her panels of guests are usually composed of neoconservatives) asked Dr. Heymann, that the demise of unionism in the U.S. had left American workers voiceless and powerless? Once again, the professor demurred. Finally, she asked Heymann what she thought American workers who want to work in conditions as good as, say, Lesotho (they've recently surpassed us), ought to do.

Her answer: write to your congressman. As if all 435 members of Congress haven't been bought and paid for many times over by corporate employers whose lobbyists won't rest until slavery has been restored and expanded to include members of every race save those lucky enough to own a company. As if the great social advances of the past, from women's suffrage to civil rights to gay rights to the twelve- (and then ten- and then eight-) hour day had been achieved as the result of politely worded letters to elected representatives. As if writing to your congressman isn't a complete fucking waste of time.

We're stuck. We've been stuck. But no one knows what to do about it. We're stuck because we have been conned into thinking that we can only work within the system. And to really get down to it, we're refusing to do the one thing that might actually work: go *outside* the system. Or, better yet—much, much better—get rid of that system entirely.

Consider the officially sanctioned alternatives available to you, Mr. or Ms. Average Angry American. Odds are that you've actually deployed most or even all of these options at one time or another:

► *Lodging a Complaint through the Media*: You can write a letter to the newspaper. You can post a blog entry. You can, as a customer of Bank of America did when the company increased the interest on her credit card to 36 percent, record an invective-filled video, post it on the Internet, and hope that it goes viral.

▶ *Marching in a Peaceful Protest*: Whether it's a war based on lies or a housing development on sacred land, you can grab a magic marker, draw up a picket sign, and head to an organized, authorized peaceful protest, or put up fliers and create one of your own. It's a proud tradition and no one can fault you for it (except the cops who might arrest you for having the wrong permit or trespassing on public property), but what are the odds of even a major protest demonstration effecting a change in policy? If the history of the post-Vietnam protest movement is any measure, slim to none.

▶ *Voting*: With the choices realistically limited to two major parties with political agendas more similar than not, both occupying a narrow spectrum on the left-to-right scale, it hardly seems worth using space to point out the obvious ineffectiveness of American-style representative democracy. Huge segments of the political spectrum (most notably anyone to the left of Bill Clinton) go entirely unrepresented. And even within the limited Democrat vs. Republican dialogue, voters get cheated in election after election. Some elections are stolen outright, as Democrats saw in Florida in 2000 and Ohio in 2004. Others are spun into irrelevance by the media, as when Obama was characterized as the liberal/progressive alternative to Hillary Rodham Clinton during the 2008 Democratic primaries (the truth may prove to be the reverse). Sometimes voters engage in mass self-delusion, as when left-of-center Democrats supported Obama—despite his remarkably honest and concise self-description as a centrist during the campaign. I like to point to two issues as examples of the pointlessness of voting: free trade and abortion. If you oppose free trade agreements, for whom are you going to vote? Both the Democrats and the Republicans favor them. If you oppose abortion, the same is true. One exception may be the direct referendum system that began in California—that's a rare example of real democracy in action—but such systems only address a tiny fraction of 1 percent of the political issues addressed in legislation each year and often support extreme-right reactionary positions.

The utter hopelessness of the American people when faced with outrageous acts of misconduct and negligence by government and business is placed in sharp relief by their letters to the editors of newspapers and other news outlets. They decry what has happened and call for accountability—but by whom? They don't say because they don't know whom to name.

"This must not be allowed to be swept under the rug,"

wrote a Michigan woman to the *New York Times* in response to what happened to Todd Willingham, the Texas man "mistakenly" murdered by the state, which then covered up the circumstances of his trial, appeal, and execution. "There must be an accounting of how Texas allowed this innocent man to be murdered by the state, and those who are responsible for this must be punished to the fullest extent of the law."[65] Note the letter writer's passive tone. It never occurred to her that power never polices itself. When powerful figures like a governor subvert what is right, who can prosecute him? Only the people. Only in the streets.

A New Yorker also wrote, voicing his dismay: "How is it that the prosecutors who so recklessly pushed this case and others like it can't be charged with negligent homicide?" he asked. "That certainly is what they are guilty of. At least they should be seriously liable for enormous civil damages. Why hasn't anyone tried this approach?"[66]

Someone should do *something*. But who?

In old Texas a century ago or in rural Pakistan today, the friends and relatives of an innocent man who was convicted by a stupid jury that relied on the testimony of unqualified expert witnesses, and was then executed by a feckless governor who subsequently tried to cover up the injustice, would likely have settled things themselves. Back then, Willingham's friends and relatives would have turned vigilante and mopped up the evildoers. Vigilantism is out of style now, and rightfully so, but one has to wonder whether Texas Governor Rick Perry would have acted as callously and corruptly as he did in the Willingham case were the mores of the Old West still in practice today.

Similarly, it's amazing that the executives of coal companies who have deliberately dumped toxins into water consumed by more than twenty million people sleep soundly at night. None need worry about retribution for their actions. Their victims all subscribe to the same vague old credo: why doesn't someone do something?

"The companies that pollute our environment and our food won't pay for the damage they've done," wrote a man to the *New York Times* after it ran a report about the poisoning in West Virginia. "It is the government's job in this country to protect its people."[67] Indeed it is. But the government won't do anything unless the people force it to. And writing a letter to a newspaper doesn't qualify as doing something.

Unless you're hopelessly self-deluded or stupid, you have to accept the painful truth. Under the current triumvirate of state power currently presiding over our lives—governmental, corporate, and media—you have no more ability to change anything important—e.g. the way the economy is managed, or which countries and people are being attacked by the armies you pay for—than a medieval serf or a German under Nazism did in the past, or a detainee in a CIA secret prison somewhere does now.

Protesters marched in Copenhagen and other cities during the 2009 climate change conference. Many wore masks over their mouths; they were printed with the slogans "clean the air" and "reduce emissions." I don't know which was less effective: the wimpy tone of the requests (how about "eliminate pollution"?) or the symbolism of the masks themselves, which have become common at marches concerning any number of issues. Environmentalists are effectively silenced by the corporate media. Why remain mute in the streets, too? Most telling was a photo of a sit-down protest in Oslo. Clean-cut men and women sat politely, holding signs that read: "Obama: Our Planet. Your Decision." Talk about impotence! If it's our planet, isn't it—isn't everything—up to us? To *all* of us?

You can pen a wistful letter to the editor: "Golly, it sure would be keen if someone [someone *else* because I am scared or simply don't have any spare time to squander on pointless campaigns] were to get off his ass and do something." You can make noise. You can Twitter. You can post on Facebook. You can chant as you march down the street of your favorite liberal-minded urban center. ("The people, united, will never be defeated!" Sure they will.) But you have no (real) voice unless you stand up and act, because the person who should do something is *you*, and millions like you. There is nobody else.

NOT EVEN ON THE LEFT

The leftist economics magazine *Dollars & Sense* recently editorialized about the surprising docility of the American working class despite the shitty economy. Historically, economic depressions have led to political unrest: new unions, strikes, even revolutions. But not this time. Not here. Why not? wondered the editors.

"On the same day in late January [2009]," they noted, "two separate public radio programs featured multiple interviews with ordinary Americans who had lost their jobs. How were they coping? What did they plan to do to repair the damage the recession had done to their lives?"[68]

Notice, even in a "socialist" magazine, the unconscious acceptance of the terms and politically loaded descriptions used by government and pro-government media spin doctors: "recession." By any standard economic definition, the crisis of 2008-to-whenever was far more severe than a recession. Such is the insidious role of the official Left in America: as vested in the continuation of the system as the *New York Times*, the very existence of such government-sanctioned media outlets perpetuates and validates the status quo they pretend to critique.

Dollars & Sense portrayed confused middle-class Americans as maintaining a stiff upper lip while the economic chaos destroyed their quality of life. It was poignant. It was also revealing. "The unemployed guests and callers were nearly all managing to stay chin-up and optimistic, though all acknowledged some fear. Many shared creative strategies for staying afloat. One person was picking up odd jobs while looking for contract work in Iraq. Another invented a board game about the frustrations of job hunting. Another was helping to build a barter network so people could get some of the things they need without cash. Some were starting small businesses—a social networking website for laid-off tech workers, an organic farm."

U.S. occupation troops have detained twenty-four hundred children in Iraq, including some as young as ten, since 2003. —Human Rights Watch, May 2008[69]

Why is the person in search of "contract work in Iraq"— in other words, direct voluntary participation in the economic exploitation of a country brutalized by twenty years of American military attacks, now under the heel of a military occupation that most Americans, including the sitting president during his election campaign, declare to be illegal and immoral—allowed to escape opprobrium in a left-wing magazine? Even if one were inclined to be charitable to a man willing to serve as a cog in such a depraved endeavor as the raping of U.S.-occupied Iraq (which I am not), one should at least expect such phraseology as: "One person was so desperate for work that he was considering searching for work in Iraq." This is a second example, in a short piece in a magazine that by American standards is a laudable and important critic of U.S. government policy, of journalistic Stockholm syndrome. No doubt the editors never intended to legitimize the Iraq war. Yet they did.

The *Dollars & Sense* editorial continues:

> You have to admire the gumption of people who keep on smiling—and looking for work—a year or even two post-layoff. On an individual level, keeping up that get-up-and-go may be the most important thing to do . . . But curiously, no one mentioned two of the most obvious (at least to us) responses to the economic crisis: getting angry and getting organized. The solutions were mostly individual, in a few cases communal—but never political. That individual orientation is evident, too, in the dearth of political protest over the daily litany of abuse, corruption and greed on the part of corporate big-wigs and their politician friends. In the United States, that is. Elsewhere around the globe, protest is rife: from Guadeloupe to China, people are organizing factory sit-ins, mass public demonstrations, and general strikes.

It's tempting to blame Americans for their troubles—particularly their willingness to sit there and take it while getting fucked over, while "get-up-and-go" foreigners are kicking government and business ass. But American workers know there's a leadership problem: there are few unions militant enough to take over a factory. Pissed-off taxpayers who don't want trillions of dollars' worth of their money going to rapacious banks like Goldman Sachs and the American International Group insurance outfit know that the difference in outcome between marching in front of their headquarters in Manhattan and staying home is nonexistent. A general strike? Wouldn't there first have to be a real American opposition party or coalition to organize it? Americans don't rebel for the same reason most of them don't vote: in a closed system controlled by two parties, it doesn't accomplish anything.

I got laid off in April 2009. I was an executive-editor at a media corporation called United Feature Syndicate. (United is the company that makes sure that what's left of your newspaper includes "Peanuts" reruns and "Marmaduke" on what's left of its comics page.) It was, as getting fired usually is, a dismal experience. My boss, Lisa, had been trying to harass me into quitting for months: insulting me at meetings in front of my colleagues ("why don't you do your *job*, Ted?"), assigning me Herculean tasks she knew I couldn't perform ("develop a turnkey solution for all newspapers, everywhere"—

huh?), attempting to humiliate me by making me do shit work previously assigned to entry-level employees. When the layoffs came, everyone knew the ax was about to fall. I assumed I'd be on Lisa's hit list. As a friend who had been through the process before had predicted, she called and asked, "Ted? Would you step into my office for a minute?" I spied the human resources lady and took grim satisfaction in the fact that I'd outlasted Lisa's campaign to make me quit—and would therefore qualify for unemployment benefits.

But I was also angry. Aside from the way I'd been treated, the "separation agreement" the company told me I would have to sign if I wanted my crappy four weeks severance payment required that I agree to never "disparage"—that is, diss—United. I was prepared to agree to that.

They also wanted me—ridiculous but true—to agree to never work for any media company again. Ever. For the rest of my life.

In other words, I would have had to quit drawing political cartoons. And my column. Publishing this book would have been a breach of contract! United refused to budge—the assholes kept repeating a meaningless, nonlegal phrase: "reduction in force." Some company lawyer had decreed that all their layoff victims would have to agree to sign the same deal. They wouldn't change a word. "Don't worry about it," the human resources lady told me. "They won't enforce it." Not having been born yesterday,

I had no choice. I turned it down. I walked away without a cent.

To whom could I have turned to wage disgruntled-former-employee *jihad* against E. W. Scripps? (Scripps is the parent company of United Media, of which United Feature Syndicate is a fully owned subsidiary.) As at most "white-collar" companies, there is no union at E. W. Scripps. So much for taking over the office and kicking out Lisa and her fellow bosses while militant workers burst into the sweet strains of "The Internationale."

I called a few lawyers. Legally, they informed me, I didn't have a leg to stand on. Like most Americans, my employment contract categorized me as an "at will" employee. In the United States employers can hire and fire anyone they want, for any reason, unless they're dumb enough to do so for reasons of race, gender, or other legally unsanctioned forms of discrimination and are so dumb that they let that fact become known by the fired worker. Interestingly, in France and other countries, "at will" employment is rare. Even low-level workers receive employment contracts and are, as a result, difficult to fire unless the employer can demonstrate consistently bad performance.

According to my attorneys, the courts had repeatedly ruled that contracts that contain sweeping prohibitions against earning a living like the one United Media offered me were unenforceable. So I could sue to challenge the terms of the severance agreement. I would have probably won, but the costs of bringing a lawsuit to trial would almost certainly have exceeded the pittance they were offering as severance.

So much for legal action. But there was another option.

Unlike almost anyone else who finds himself out of a job, I had direct access to the media. Not only am I a syndicated editorial cartoonist, I write a column that goes out to dozens of daily and weekly newspapers and their websites around the world. I could have enumerated my litany of complaints in my column. It would have annoyed the hell out of Lisa and her boss (which could only have served the greater good). It would have appeared everywhere from the *Tampa Tribune* to the *Japan Times* in Tokyo to the opinion section of Yahoo! News, where I am routinely read by millions of discrete/unique visitors, as they say in the Web world. But while publishing such a rant would have made me walk around my studio with a big ol' smarmy grin on my face for a day or two, it would have accomplished nothing whatsoever from a material standpoint. E. W. Scripps wouldn't have backed down. I wouldn't have gotten my severance. I certainly wouldn't have gotten my job back.

No government agency, no lawyer, no editor, no union, no one could or would help me in any way whatsoever. I knew that. Not under the current system. Like the other ten-plus million American workers who got canned since the not-so-great depression began, I was alone.

DON'T COUNT ON THE OFFICIAL LEFT

Liberal agent non-provocateur and filmmaker Michael Moore embodies the zeitgeist of our system: Capitalism today in America recognizes the mortal danger that it, and thus we, are in and channels it into a wholesome, profit-generating product meant to reassure its audience that the mere fact that we can talk about our problems means we'll muddle through somehow. With the best of intentions, Moore is the best the official Left has to offer. No other mainstream progressive personality is as effective, passionate, or widely disseminated as Moore. His failings, therefore, embody what's wrong with the American Left.

Dangerous times, like the present, lead to dangerous ideas. But dangerous ideas are best expressed as safely as possible. And so 2009 spawned Moore's documentary film *Capitalism: A Love Story*, billed as a "multi-pronged argument against a system that [Moore] contends is fundamentally corrupt and undemocratic."[70]

If a system is "fundamentally corrupt and undemocratic," it follows that it should be abolished posthaste. But Moore can't/won't say that. Moore's "argument" can't/doesn't call for armed revolution, or communism, or, really, anything at all. A few weeks after his film was released, CNN's Wolf Blitzer asked the director what he thought about President Obama. "I still like him," said Moore. "I'm rooting for him." In other words, the director and writer of a film declaring capitalism immoral and dictatorial is "rooting" for the head of state of the nation most responsible for propagating that system and who came to office as the direct result of its intrinsically undemocratic political process—and whose economic policies are obsessively pro-capitalist.

What's amazing about this rancid little system of ours is that most of its cogs have no idea they play a key role in keeping it going. In an interview, Moore asserts (and I believe him) that this was the film he had always been working up the courage to produce. He thinks he's dangerous. He believes that the powers-that-be have it out for him and his radical message.

"I've been thinking about this film for probably about twenty years," Moore told an interviewer for the A/V Club section of the satirical weekly newspaper the *Onion*. The A/V Club is the straightforward, pop-culture/movies/music section of the otherwise sarcastic-to-a-fault paper, which serves as the print equivalent of Jon Stewart, Stephen Colbert, and Bill Maher on cable television. It allows powerless Americans to rejoice in the ridicule of their oppressors, who couldn't possibly feel less threatened.

These things can make your head hurt.

Still, you have to love the A/V Club. They ask the tough questions, the ones Fox News doesn't dream of. "If you're sympathetic to its message," the interviewer asked Moore, "*Capitalism* is a film that's likely to leave people angry over various injustices, but short of revolution, what can people do? What is the takeaway from the film?"

Here is Moore's complete answer: "Well, the first thing is, they're going to walk out of the theater knowing more than when they walked in. I'm going to show them things they haven't seen, I'm going to tell them things they haven't heard. I'm going to expose them to ideas that for some reason aren't discussed on the cable shows or the op-ed pieces."

Moore doesn't question the interviewer's premise: that a solution should *fall short of revolution*. Why *shouldn't* we have a revolution? Isn't it obvious that nothing short of revolution can fix a system impervious to reform? It certainly hasn't worked in Moore's lifetime.

Fix-from-within solutions are inherently doomed. The reason is simple: no one gives up power voluntarily. The rulers of oppressive regimes have even less motivation to give up control than those who run other types of government; tyrants rightly fear the retribution of the liberated.

The United States of America is one of the most internally and externally violent societies to have ever existed, yet liberal critics of its government and corporate policies like Moore continuously try to reform them by deploying satire. Whether it's political cartoonists, liberal-minded television comedians like Jon Stewart and Stephen Colbert, or culture jammers like Andy Bichlbaum and Mike

Bonanno, their efforts are doomed from the outset. They end up strengthening the regime by legitimizing it.

As the Yes Men, Bichlbaum and Bonanno pull pranks against evil companies, impersonating officials from Dow Chemical as they "apologize" and issue (fraudulent) pledges of financial restitution to the long-suffering victims of the disaster in Bophal, India. (Dow purchased Union Carbide, the company responsible.) They take the government to task by pretending to represent the U.S. Department of Housing and Urban Development and promising to finally help the victims of Katrina.

Liberal fans like the Yes Men because they're funny and because they expose the absurdities and internal contradictions of the capitalist system. Yet there's a sinister subtext to their brand of satire: the mere fact that it's (sort of) allowed, that it is distributed in small arts theaters and via Netflix gives hope that the system can be reformed without violent change. The same can be said of capitalism and the particular brand of corporate-governmental-media synergy running things today—and that's no coincidence. They are one and the same. To take on the system, one must reject it.

Russell Peterson, an American studies professor and a former political cartoonist, puts it well: "In spite of the fact that comedy about politics is now as common as crabgrass, political comedy—that is, genuine satire, which uses comedic means to advance a serious critique—is so rare we might be tempted to conclude it is extinct . . . Election after election, night after night, joke after joke, they have reinforced the notion that political participation is pointless, parties and candidates are interchangeable, and democracy is futile."

(There is genuine satire. And it works. But you won't find it in mainstream media.)

Like other liberal critics of the regime, Michael Moore is probably scared. And rightly so! Were he to declare himself in favor of a revolution or something less, something vaguer ("radical change," let's say), Moore would soon find himself marginalized by the media to an even greater extent than he is today. Were he to continue to express opinions too far outside the "mainstream"—in other words, unacceptable to the corporate-controlled media—his films might no longer find widespread distribution. He could lose money, prestige, and—to give him the benefit of the doubt, to assume that he really does want to change things—the ability to get his message out to the people. So he ends up exemplifying America at its worst instead. In the guise of inciting us to action, he turns us into couch potatoes watching reality television.

I'm scared, too. Government spooks read our e-mail, listen to our telephone conversations, and employ data-mining techniques in order to learn everything they can about us, our private lives, and personal thoughts. They spend more time and energy going after lefties than

Islamist terrorists. Imagine my surprise when I learned that the New York Police Department and other government agencies were tapping my phones and monitoring my activities. It was scary. It was also ridiculous: "Undercover officers attended meetings of political groups, posing as sympathizers or fellow activists, and infiltrated chat rooms," reported the *New York Times* on May 16, 2007. There was "a Nov. 13, 2003 [NYPD] digest noting the Web site of the editorial cartoonist and activist Ted Rall. 'Activists are talking, some with barely hidden glee, about the possibility of violence,' [at the 2004 Republican National Convention in New York] an officer wrote, describing postings on Mr. Rall's site."[71]

Poor cops . . . they must be seriously bored.

E UNUM PLURIBUS: ON OUR OWN, AND MISERABLE

Many people think they can avoid being targeted by the state. All they have to do to be safe is be white, and rich or middle class. But they are mistaken.

You are mistaken. The state is already at war with you. All I'm asking you to do is fight back.

Well-off white folks may not get pulled over due to the color of their skin, get shot by trigger-happy cops, or be forced to watch their kids vomit blood after they drink contaminated drinking water. But the system attacks "normal," "average" people just the same. Unless you belong to the elite fraction of 1 percent of Americans whose wealth and connections make them close to untouchable, you are routinely victimized and abused by a government whose sole objectives are preserving itself and big business.

I am white and male and Ivy League–educated, yet even I have been falsely arrested and subjected to police brutality. If there is a person who can live out his or her natural lifespan without being the victim of state violence in one form or another, I have yet to hear of him. Insurance companies cheat their customers out of claims, killing many and dooming countless more to flagging health. Employers brazenly violate the law—did you know, for example, that all full-time workers (who do not directly supervise other workers) are entitled to overtime pay? Unfairness and injustice abound. There is nowhere to appeal.

Those who write their congressmen get form letters in return. The Better Business Bureau has stopped collecting complaints. The Chamber of Commerce doesn't give a rat's ass. After I was mistreated by the Los Angeles Police Department, I filed a complaint with the Internal Affairs Division. What a joke! No one called. It was categorically dismissed. I expected this. Non-responsiveness is the rule nowadays. Injustice is normative.

In a study of the Chicago Police Department examining more than ten thousand complaints of abuse filed between 2002 and 2004, only nineteen resulted in meaningful disciplinary action. *E unum pluribus*—we're all on our own.

Responsibility has been diffused to the extent that protest marchers, were anyone motivated to carry a picket sign, are hard pressed to know whom or what to demonstrate against, or even where to demonstrate. The tools of state and corporate repression have become airtight, approaching 100 percent efficiency in their ability to evade the slightest consequence of their actions. Pity the disgruntled layoff victim with a gun and a grudge. Whom should he shoot? His supervisor? The president? The president of the parent company? Or the faceless analyst at the consulting firm that recommended eliminating his position?

Society has become ruthlessly automated. Breeze through a traffic signal—or, more precisely, trigger a preprogrammed response—and a camera captures your license plate. Optical recognition software reads the numbers, crosschecks a national database, and automatically generates a ticket, which (assuming you haven't moved since the last time you renewed your license) is mailed to you.

High-tech automation only works in one direction: against you. Assuming you can obtain a phone number for the ticketing agency, the line is busy. Or you're kept on hold before being disconnected. Perhaps you're dumped into voicemail; if the in-box isn't full, there is next to no chance that anyone will ever return your call. You could take a day off work to challenge the ticket. But what are your chances of prevailing? Even if you're innocent? It's easier to pay. Even after your check clears (or, if you're younger, you grant the state access to your bank account so it can be automatically debited along with a fee), the computerized security state keeps attacking you. All fifty states and U.S. territories and possessions automatically receive the information that you have pled guilty to a traffic violation. In some states, extra "points" on your license may prompt the Department of Motor Vehicles to suspend your driving privileges—even if it's in a state that never issued you a driving permit. You may have a California driver license, with a driving record that does not warrant your privileges to be changed or reduced in that state. Unbeknownst to you, New York State may have declared you a suspended driver. If you get pulled over in New York, you will be arrested, taken to jail, and fined thousands of dollars.

Injustice is a fact of life in every nation at every time. What makes a government viable is the perception that there is a mechanism to redress wrongdoing by the state once it comes to light. No regime, including those that rule through naked fear and totalitarian methods of control, can survive forever without being responsive to its citizenry. We should actually, of course, tell the state what to do.

In the U.S., the illusion of responsiveness has vanished. People who speak out at city council meetings against a planned real estate development notice that the fix is already in—the councilmen vote in favor of the developers despite community opposition. If a person suffered one of the worst crimes a state can commit against one of its citizens— imprisonment for an offense he didn't commit—there used to be a multimillion dollar jury payout to look forward to. During the past decade most states have passed laws capping damage awards for prosecutorial misconduct to small sums, typically about ten thousand dollars for each year behind bars. There's no accountability.

During the months before the American invasion of Iraq, *millions* of people marched in cities across the country and around the world to protest the looming war—but it made no difference. The tanks went in right on schedule. Four years later, more than a million Iraqis and Americans were dead. Within existing legal strictures, there is nothing the American people could have done to stop that war.

Tens of millions of peaceful marchers would have been ignored.

Only peaceful protest is considered legitimate, but it is clear to anyone who pays attention that peaceful protest, carried out with the permission of an official parade permit, doesn't work. So the apathetic slob who sits at home playing video games is no less effective than the politically conscious activist who schedules her life around protest marches.

As everyone knows from firsthand experience, here, in "the land of the free and the home of the brave," state-sanctioned robbers act with impunity. In recent years, health insurance companies and credit card issuers have been especially outrageous. It is widely known that the refusal of medical insurers to cover people with "pre-existing conditions" and to pay out perfectly legitimate claims leads to the deaths of at least forty-four thousand Americans each year. Many more suffer needlessly because the system intentionally refuses to provide the service—prompt reimbursement of doctor's bills and medications—for which customers pay as much as one thousand dollars per month. Credit card companies and banks are universally reviled. Even after they received billions of federal tax dollars to save them from bankruptcy, banks continued to collect billions more from consumers in the form of usurious overdraft fees and double-digit interest rate charges—some as high as 40 percent, many around 20 percent. The same banks pay out a paltry 1 percent on savings accounts.

People are angry. Yet nothing changes. Why should it? It won't happen unless we force the issue.

"SHORT OF REVOLUTION"

In December 2009 Barack Obama traveled to Stockholm to collect the Nobel Peace Prize. Quite a few commentators were amazed by his win, given that the president had no diplomatic achievements under his belt. Moreover, he had escalated Bush's wars against Iraq and Afghanistan.

A Boston man wrote the following letter to the *New York Times*:

> The Nobel Peace Prize only underscores the irony and sadness of President Obama's Afghanistan policy. On that memorable night a year ago, in Grant Park in Chicago, before an impressed and stunned nation and world, Mr. Obama promised that change would come to America.
>
> We looked forward to change where we could become more disengaged from, and impartial about, the world's conflicts, since we are not the world's policeman. Where anti-American extremism and terrorism could begin their gradual decline and eventual disappearance because the swamp would be drained of motivation for them.
>
> But to our disappointment we find the recycled and failed policies of Lyndon B. Johnson, George W. Bush and Secretary of Defense Donald H. Rumsfeld.
>
> All we can do now is hold out hope that change will come to Mr. Obama himself, that he will reinvent us as a nation newly disengaged from conflict,

where hatred against America can become virtually extinct, where we can at last make our peace with the world.[72]

Nicely stated. But with such passivity!

Unanswered in this letter is why Obama should change his policies if no one—no one!—plans to even try to pressure him to do so.

I was astonished by the tone of an article in the *Los Angeles Times* that reported the reticence of antiwar activists to protest Obama's decision to send more army divisions to the war in Afghanistan. The problem: so many of the would-be protesters had voted for Obama. That part didn't surprise me. What did was this quote: "'People are really burned out,' explained [antiwar activist] Laurie Dobson." Burned out? From what? Eight years into the Afghan conflict, there have been few major protest demonstrations against it. Burned out from having hoped Obama would ride in and save the day, and then being bitterly disappointed when he did nothing of the kind—just as he promised during his campaign?

We must stop fooling ourselves.

Speaking of which:

The United States is over. Its economy has passed through the stage of late capitalism; it is dying. Its internal contradictions—which, like those of every system of governance, were present from the start—have finally caught up with it. Its corporate and political leaders know what must be done to keep it going, yet can't lift a finger to save themselves. As for so-called liberals like Obama, they are useless. But what about us?

We can organize. We can wait for the right moment. We can rise up.

We can get rid of this zombie system of government, which is dead in every way that matters.

III. THE OPPORTUNITY

The mass of men serve the state thus, not as men mainly, but as machines, with their bodies. They are the standing army, and the militia, jailers, constables, posse comitatus, etc. In most cases there is no free exercise whatever of the judgment or of the moral sense; but they put themselves on a level with wood and earth and stones; and wooden men can perhaps be manufactured that will serve the purpose as well. Such command no more respect than men of straw or a lump of dirt. They have the same sort of worth only as horses and dogs. Yet such as these even are commonly esteemed good citizens. Others—as most legislators, politicians, lawyers, ministers, and office-holders—serve the state chiefly with their heads; and, as they rarely make any moral distinctions, they are as likely to serve the devil, without intending it, as God. A very few—as heroes, patriots, martyrs, reformers in the great sense, and men— serve the state with their consciences also, and so necessarily resist it for the most part; and they are commonly treated as enemies by it.

—Henry David Thoreau, Resistance to Civil Government, 1848

Ironically, the very somnolence that defines American apathy—as long as people have enough food and there are five hundred channels on cable television, they don't give a damn who their government bombs or tortures—means that a revolutionary crisis is *more* likely in the United States than it might be under similar circumstances elsewhere. People don't have to hit objective rock bottom; they merely have to feel that they have.

Things are worse in Zimbabwe than they will probably ever become here, but dictator Robert Mugabe has yet to face a serious political challenge. Sadly, Zimbabweans are accustomed to a level of poverty and governmental malfeasance that you or I could hardly imagine.

Growing up in the world's sole remaining superpower, Americans have long enjoyed access to a quality of life (in terms of consumer products, not social services) with few equals in the world. Losing the wherewithal to pay for the quality of life they are used to, due to a depression triggered by a hard-to-understand subprime mortgage meltdown, will be a huge shock to many Americans. Like citizens of the former USSR, which also had first-world living standards, we will not accept downward mobility. We will be confused and angry. And we will have role models. We will watch on television as people in other countries more accustomed to revolutionary violence take to the streets and seize control of their destinies.

Before long, motivated by despair both real and imagined, both nationalistic and personal, we will do the same.

Of course, a revolutionary moment doesn't necessarily,

or even usually, lead to revolution. The United States passed through such a moment in 1968, when the assassinations of Robert F. Kennedy, Martin Luther King, and Malcolm X prompted urban riots, and the Vietnam War radicalized such groups as the Students for a Democratic Society (SDS) and the Weather Underground. Revolution didn't happen then. The crisis passed. But things could have gone differently.

TALKING ABOUT A REVOLUTION

The economic collapse presents the American Left with a rare chance to radicalize and channel the hopes and frustrations of previously moderate people into supporting the wholesale reorganization of American society, including its economic structure. For the first time in half a century, the myths and shibboleths of gangster capitalism are crumbling.

For the first time I can remember, it is possible to criticize the basic economic underpinnings of the American political system without being instantly shouted down as a subversive, communist, socialist, or any other of the Red-baiting terms commonly used during the George W. Bush years. Certainly, right-wing talk radio hosts and the reactionary demonstrators who respond to them still shout "socialist!" They wave images of the hammer and sickle around as if they still held their former awesome, conversation-killing power. But they do not. It is now possible, in the mainstream media, to speak of socialism as a viable alternative to capitalism. Could you have imagined this five years ago?

Old lies are being abandoned. Labor statistics fraudulently manipulated to produce a false picture of widespread prosperity have been exposed by new, widely accepted terms like "broader unemployment" and "underemployment." Articles in stodgy free-market rags like the *Financial Times* and the *Wall Street Journal* now ask: "Is capitalism doomed?" (And the answer isn't an automatic "no way.") The system is being called to account across the board: "The point is that the West (capitalism) is to blame for every natural disaster in the world, all of which are now presumed to have been caused by global warming, which is presumed to have been caused by us," writes a columnist for the Toronto *Globe and Mail*.[73] (When you run everything, you get blamed when there's trouble.)

It is finally possible to say out loud what used to get lefties laughed at. A year after the financial meltdown, the *Times of India* ran an op-ed calling capitalism itself into question: "People are increasingly skeptical of capitalism not merely because of recent market failures but because they realize the limits of a politico-economic system that is driven by greed and competition. Human greed can't be the engine of progress. An economic system that needs to promote conspicuous consumption is not sustainable. In fact, such a system is a threat to the survival of this planet. As often said, there is enough to satisfy everyone's needs in this world, but not enough to satisfy everyone's greed."[74] Sing, Leninist hearts! These are the editors of the biggest English-language newspaper in the world!

The classic indicator of revolutionary crisis—dissatisfaction among the young educated elite—is at Def-Con 4. Recent college graduates, the would-have-been future technocrats and businesspeople who under normal circumstances would have revitalized and defended the system, no longer see a career path ahead. They aren't vested. They're not going to be.

It will soon become clear to the young adults of the privileged bourgeoisie that they stand to gain more from the replacement of the existing order than from its perpetuation. At this writing the official unemployment rate among young adults aged twenty to twenty-four is over 16 percent and rising—more than five points above the national average. The career center director at UCLA said that the job prospects of recent graduates were the worst of her thirty-two-year career. According to a December 2009 article in the *Los Angeles Times*, the research director of the National Association of Colleges and Employers "said he'd had discussions with several dozen colleges in recent weeks, and some of them are seeing employment rates as low as thirty percent for those who graduated six or seven months ago." The article quoted a twenty-two-year-old UCLA graduate: "I have very few friends who are employed. Even friends who are . . . they're taking temporary jobs just to pay rent."[75]

Seventy percent unemployment among recent college graduates is not a prescription for political stability.

Mainstream media personalities on corporate-owned television networks openly discuss socialism as an alternative—not a viable or desirable alternative, exactly, but still, as a system worthy of legitimate discussion. This is their way of letting off steam, of venting anger, of serving as a sort of official opposition within the official party line. It's the same reason the Party invented an opposition in George Orwell's *1984*. Then, the phony resistance of Oceania helped create a real one.

As *Forbes* magazine noted in March 2009: "Carefully constructed national social pacts are highly vulnerable to this economic crisis. These are robust during normal counter-cyclical periods but insufficiently robust during a period of mass unemployment. This political atmosphere is ripe for nationalist xenophobia and extremist political parties or movements."[76] The game has begun. The Right and Left will play for what remains after the implosion of the soon-to-be *ancien régime*.

THE LEFT-IN-WAITING

Even if one agreed with their goals and ideals, the Right is genetically disinclined to revolution. Conservatism protects the existing order, magnifies it, pushes it to be more extreme. Radical change, the ouster of one set of elites by the underclass, is anathema to rightists.

Actual revolution has to come from the Left. Unfortunately for those who dream of a fairer, more egalitarian, less militaristic and expansionist United States, there is no actual left. There is certainly no organized, capital-L left to speak of.

The mainstream Democratic Party, a party that would be deemed center-right in Europe, marginalized and expelled its liberal wing during the 1980s and 1990s, falling under the sway of the Clintons' "centrist" (that is, conservative) Democratic Leadership Council. Old-school 1960s-era liberals still turn out for elections. But they have switched from activism to obstructionism, (unsuccessfully) begging Democratic officials to resist the Republican Right's initiatives.

Labor unions, co-opted by the "team management" approach of the 1980s, have been seduced onto the boards of the corporations whose employees they are supposed to be representing. They abandoned militancy long ago, purging members whose left-of-center viewpoints brought class analysis to their dealings with management. When former AFL-CIO chairman Lane Kirkland died in 1999, the caption under the photo accompanying his *Wall Street Journal* obituary read "anti-communist."

As for bona fide radical left and communist groups,

they are tiny, factionalized, and poorly organized. They devote most of their energies to fundraising by selling their newspapers on college campuses.

America has no left.

America does have a left-in-waiting: academics, pundits, musicians, publishers, and activist groups that seek to create alternative realities to the status quo. People and grassroots organizations like Democracy Now, Noam Chomsky, Ward Churchill, Jello Biafra, Project Censored, Teaching for Change, AK Press, Common Dreams, and thousands of other people and places and institutions could supply participants or be participants themselves in a rebellion and subsequent reconstruction.

But they are not a real left. The cells of such a left must be created. Next they must mutate and coalesce into a fast-moving organism. Such cells can receive both tacit and overt support from the left-in-waiting. A real left exists in the hopes and dreams of all Americans who know in their hearts what is possible, but haven't dared speak up because doing so would mean being alone, ridiculed, and possibly worse. It is time for the real Left to step out of the realm of the imaginary.

America also has a proletariat-in-waiting: tens of millions of people who have given up on the system. (Whether they ever believed in it in the first place is doubtful.) African Americans, illegal immigrants, and other oppressed racial minorities have been biding their time, waiting for white

America to, depending on their point of view, create an opportunity or come to its collective senses. Alienated, dispossessed, and beyond disgusted, blacks will certainly assume a major role in any future uprising. One may hope that their actions will be directed toward the plutocrats and corrupt political personalities and governmental bodies responsible for our collective ruination. But we may get a race war instead. Once the dogs of revolution are loosed, anything can happen—but that's a chance that we will have to take.

The revolutionary potential of women is an open question. On the one hand, women remain oppressed by patriarchy. They earn 20 percent less than men and are disproportionately victims of violence. One only has to observe the sea of white male faces at a joint session of Congress or a gathering of corporate chiefs, not to mention the fact that there has never been a female presidential nominee, much less president, to understand the secondary status of women in American society. But, as Kathy McAfee and Myrna Wood noted in their influential 1969 essay "Bread and Roses": "More often than not [women's liberation groups] never get beyond the level of therapy sessions; rather than aiding the political development of women and building a revolutionary women's movement, they often encourage escape from political struggle . . . A movement organized by women around the oppression of women . . . is bound to emphasize the bourgeois and personal aspects of oppression and to obscure the material oppression of working class women and men."[77] The feminist movement "lacks revolutionary potential" argued Bernadine Dohrn, then of Students for a Democratic Society, later the Weather Underground.

Certainly, women will and should be equal partners in revolutionary change with their male comrades. From a practical standpoint, however, it is likely that male anger—because men feel especially disempowered economically and politically—will prove more combustible.

Consider "the boy problem": male students are underachieving at a staggering rate. Nationally, 57 percent of college undergraduates are women. Not that women aren't suffering from the current Depression, but unemployment and depressed wages have hit men much harder than women. There's at least a 2-percent gap between the unemployment rates for men and women, in favor of the latter.

The less you have to lose, the more likely you are to be willing to overturn the apple cart. Millions of men have lost everything—and it's not coming back unless they fight to take it back.

A tool of the permanent underclass will be, ironically, one facet of our individualistic mythos: contempt for authority. Blacks hate cops more than whites do, but whites also loathe them; in the tony suburbs where I often find myself driving I witness acts of civil disobedience that you've seen too. Perhaps you've never considered the implications: The driver of a car passing you in the opposite direction flashes his high beams, then turns them off. Up the road, you come across a police cruiser. The message is quintessentially antiauthoritarian: "Watch out: cop ahead. Slow down. Be careful."

They wouldn't do that if they thought you had just robbed a store or kidnapped a child. People do it because they dislike the police. They hate cops because they've had bad experiences with them—an unfair ticket, perhaps, or a ticket whose penalty they thought was draconian. As agents of the state seen more often than any other, cops and how they're viewed tell you a lot about how people feel about their government.

Americans despise their government. So what comes next?

If the United States is to avoid the fate of the Soviet republics after independence—gangster capitalism, narcostates, rising religious fanaticism, spreading poverty as a tiny cabal of violent, well-connected elites loot what's left of the national pantry—it needs an organized left to channel the rage of the soon-to-be dispossessed into a revolutionary organization. Such a left could emerge from the chaos of collapse, but only if it is first inspired by an intellectual framework, a clear and concise set of ideas of what American society should look like after the old system dies.

There are many righteous causes for revolution in the United States: environmental degradation; violations of the rights of minorities, gays, and other victims of discrimination; the rabid militarism which has kept the country in a state of constant war despite rarely having been threatened, much less attacked, by a foreign power.

However, only the fight for economic equality can cut across cultural divides and parochial interests to unite the majority of Americans. Only hunger (and fear of the same) will be able to bring together the critical mass of mutually self-interested and motivated people necessary to overthrow the decaying republic and replace it with one that serves them. At the root of economically motivated revolution will be people's newfound unwillingness to tolerate more than a certain amount of wealth aggregation in the hands of a few. Primal law kicks in: I am starving. My friends are, too. That man has enough to feed all of us. First, we will ask him to share. If he refuses, we will take it by force. If he resists, we will kill him.

The disparity of wealth and income between the wealthiest Americans and the rest of us continues to accelerate. A 2009 study by the University of California at Berkeley showed that the top 10 percent of wage earners received nearly 50 percent of all national income, "a level," said economist Emmanuel Saez, "higher than any other year since records began in 1917 . . . that even surpasses 1928, the peak of the stock market bubble in the 'roaring' 1920s."[78] According to Charles Hurst, author of *Social Inequality: Forms, Causes, and Consequences*, the top 10 percent of Americans possess 80 percent of the nation's financial wealth. The top four hundred taxpayers in the United States had gross household incomes of at least eighty-seven million dollars in 2005, the most recent year data was available. *Forbes* lists 360 American billionaires. When the wealthy lose their pet policemen and hungry/angry/desperate people roam the streets, there will be a reckoning.

Between 1992 and 2007, America's four hundred richest households increased their average income by 399 percent, while the bottom 90 percent of the country's households gained 13 percent.
—*Los Angeles Times*, February 24, 2010[79]

Does it have to be about money? Why isn't the death-in-progress of the life-sustaining natural world (which will soon cause major food and water shortages, not to mention natural disasters like sea-level rises and coastal cities being abandoned as happened in New Orleans post-Katrina) also a major motivation for revolutionary action?

Historical precedent suggests yes; revolution is always motivated by economics. And the fiscal crisis is what people have on their minds.

In the medium-to-long run, perhaps, the murder of the planet by a small cabal of voracious industrialists will become humanity's top priority. For the time being, the threat remains abstract to the vast majority of people. In the same way that an educated person who smokes or drives too fast knows that her behavior will eventually kill her but doesn't stop because eventually doesn't equal soon, much less now, few people currently grasp how imminent environmental catastrophe really is. Environmental concerns typically poll fourth or fifth on lists of Americans' top worries. A 2009 Gallup poll asked people which should take precedence: the economy or the environment? (It's a false choice. But it shows how pollsters want to train people to think.) Forty-two percent said the environment; 51 percent the economy.[80] Despite Al Gore's *An Inconvenient Truth* and thousands of news accounts documenting environmental deterioration caused by pollution and human-caused climate change, the numbers are worse than they used to be. In 1985, the environment won hands down, 65 to 28 percent.

As the economy deteriorates, simple self-interest will overcome the bourgeoisification of the American working class, the phenomenon that causes people at all wage levels to identify themselves as middle class. (A 2008 Pew poll found that 91 percent of Americans consider themselves middle class. Two percent said they were upper class, 6 percent lower class.[81]) The traditional Marxist appeal to an American proletariat fails at least in part because no one considers themselves to belong to it. Class unconsciousness is our national religion. But that's going to change. You can't consider yourself "middle class" after the sheriff evicts you from your home. Or when your kids are hungry.

SHOCK, ANGER, DENIAL, DENIAL, DENIAL

In most other countries, at most times in recorded human history, anger manifests itself in violence. Americans are angry. Yet they haven't taken up arms. Why not?

They certainly have good cause.

In March 2009 the American International Group (AIG), which had just collected more than 170 billion dollars in federal bailout money, announced that it planned to pay 165 million dollars in bonuses to, as the *New York Times* put it, "executives in the same business unit that brought the company to the brink of collapse last year."[82] Around the same time, consumers began howling about egregious overdraft fees levied by Bank of America, Wells Fargo, and other institutions bailed out by the Bush-Obama rescue package. Charging thirty-five-dollar overdraft fees for going as little as six dollars into the red is big business, bringing in 29 billion dollars in revenue into U.S. banks in 2007—more than total sales for appliances or books nationwide. Everyone hates his bank. Everyone hates AIG. Yet neither Edward Liddy, the government-appointed chairman of AIG, and Ken Lewis, then the chief executive officer of Bank of America, had to worry about angry mobs dragging them out of their beds at night.

Which, when you think about it, is surprising. There are four guns for every man, woman, and child in the United States. For the most part, however, gun violence is limited to domestic disputes and territorial battles between rival drug dealers. Why don't the friends and relatives of Todd Willingham, unjustly murdered by the state of Texas, go after those they deem responsible? Why do parents in West Virginia wait patiently by the phone for calls from their attorneys—rather than take out a few mining company executives? Six million Americans face home foreclosure at this writing. Why are they quietly packing up and leaving?

There is anger. But it comes from the political right. It is banal, unfocused, and incoherent. And it is self-contradictory. A September 2009 Rasmussen poll found that two-thirds of Americans described themselves as angry at the policies of the federal government. Broken down by party registration, more than 90 percent of Republicans— but just 44 percent of Democrats—were pissed off.[83]

You'd think right-wingers would be happy. Obama's policies are mostly continuations of right-wing programs initiated by the previous Republican administration: the wars against Afghanistan and Iraq, bailing out large corporations, tax cuts for the wealthiest Americans, reneging on public-funded healthcare reform. But conservatives are not satisfied. Thus the Tea Party movement, which took shape (after the fact) around opposition to the bank bailouts and Obama's attempt to reform healthcare, now sputters, flailing, shaking its fists at television cameras.

Interestingly, those who tell pollsters that they are the angriest are said to be the least concerned about an outbreak of violence. The Right values law and order. Even those that crush them.

Americans worry about the possibility of political violence more than it actually occurs. Before the November 2008 presidential contest between Republican John McCain and Democrat Barack Obama, pundits and police officials predicted the possibility of riots regardless of which candidate won. "If [Obama] is elected, like with sports championships, people may go out and riot," said Bob Parks, a columnist and black Republican candidate for state representative in Massachusetts, a few weeks before the balloting. "If Barack Obama loses there will be another large group of people who will assume the election was stolen from him . . . This will be an opportunity for people who want to commit mischief."[84] In fact, nothing happened—which probably should have been expected, given the absence of action in the streets during the November–December 2000 Florida recount crisis, when millions of Al Gore supporters believed the presidential election had been stolen by Bush.

Though not as widespread as in more than eighty other countries throughout the twentieth century, domestically-originated political violence in the United States occurred in sporadic, spectacular spasms until the mid-1990s. (The 1992 race riots in Los Angeles which followed the acquittals of the police officers who beat Rodney King and the Oklahoma City bombing in 1995 were the last major acts of domestically originated political violence in the United States.)

Fifteen years later, political violence has all but disappeared, limited mostly to damage to private property. Many would hesitate to elevate vandalism to the level of genuine violence. What few actions we have seen have been carried out by antifree trade protesters and radical environmentalists. Riots following protests against the 1999 meeting of the World Trade Organization became known as "the Battle of Seattle." But they weren't serious.

Anarchists let the air out of the tires of police vehicles. Several businesses, including a Starbucks, suffered broken windows. "Two or three people went in; many bags of coffee came out, on to the street. Starbucks was being trashed," reported the BBC. "To be fair to the crowd though, most did not engage in this attack and in fact most of the coffee house was undamaged."[85] A revolution it wasn't: no one was seriously injured, much less killed. In September 2009, a year into the global economic meltdown, anti-globalization demonstrators marching against the G-20 summit in Pittsburgh tried to roll a dumpster into a line of riot policemen. Environmentalists set sports utility vehicles on fire at a car dealership; others burned empty houses at a controversial development site in Washington State. Several universities reported break-ins and acts of vandalism by animal rights activists.

That's about it.

Weigh this docile populace against the towering mountain of monstrous injustice and oppression unleashed by the ruling class against the rest of us during the last decade:

- ▶ In 2000, the U.S. Supreme Court conspired with the Republican Party to throw the presidential election (under the U.S. Constitution, federal courts don't have jurisdiction over election disputes).
- ▶ In 2001, the Bush administration used the 9/11 attacks as a pretext to ram through the USA Patriot Act, which allows the federal government to eavesdrop on telephone conversations and read electronic communications by Americans without being required to obtain a warrant.
- ▶ Also in 2001, President Bush signed an executive order granting himself the right to declare anyone, including an American citizen, an "enemy combatant" whose civil rights could be stripped and who could be ordered assassinated by order of the president or secretary of defense (the first killing under this order occurred in 2002, when the CIA

shot a missile from a Predator drone plane at an American citizen named Ahmed Hijazi).

▶ In 2002, it became public knowledge that Bush had effectively "legalized" torture and the indefinite detention of anyone, including American citizens like José Padilla and Yasser Hamdi.

▶ In 2002, Bush declared that the United States was no longer subject to the Geneva Conventions, which govern the proper treatment of prisoners of war.

▶ In 2003, the United States invaded Iraq, spending trillions of dollars and killing more than one million people, using the excuse that Iraq possessed weapons of mass destruction—a story government officials knew was untrue at the time (*Newsweek* reported that Secretary of State Colin Powell exclaimed, "I'm not reading this. This is bullshit!" about the phony intelligence reports he cited two days later during a speech at the United Nations calling for war).[86]

▶ The Military Commissions Act of 2006 attempted to strip all Americans of the centuries-old writ of habeas corpus, which guaranteed people in the Western world the right to face charges in a court of law or be released by the police in a timely manner.

▶ During the eight years of the Bush administration, the 400 richest Americans, who own more than the bottom 150 million Americans (half the population), increased their net worth by 700 billion dollars.[87]

▶ During the same eight years, the ratio of CEO pay to average pay rose from 344 to one to 525 to one.[88]

Even the assassins (Sirhan Sirhan and Lynette "Squeaky" Fromme, for example) who typically carry out attacks against political leaders have been cowed into passivity, perhaps by a seemingly omniscient security state. Despite widespread economic and personal misery, there wasn't a single serious assassination attempt by an American against President George W. Bush. The only threat occurred overseas, during a 2005 diplomatic visit to the former Soviet republic of Georgia. Vladimir Arutyunian tossed a live grenade under a podium where Bush, Georgian president Mikheil Saakashvili and their two wives were seated. The firing pin didn't deploy quickly enough, however, and the four escaped without injury.

Workplace shootings have increased, but not nearly as quickly as the outrageous behavior of employers. "In the past corporations laid off workers because business was bad," said Sam Pizzigati, associate fellow at the Institute for Policy Studies. "But over the past few decades, downsizing has been a corporate wealth-generating strategy. Today, CEOs don't spend their time making, trying to make better products: they maneuver to take over other companies, steal their customers and fire their workers."[89]

Those fired workers contribute to the 20 percent of adult Americans who are out of work.[90] They're relatively quiet now. But not for long.

"Those who make peaceful revolution impossible will make violent revolution inevitable," warned John F. Kennedy. Alternatively, as an anonymous historian remarked, "Revolution seems impossible before it happens and inevitable after it has." Both statements are true—a system that becomes rigid and unable to meet people's basic needs can only be brought down by violent over-throw—and will be. It is only a matter of how and when.

THE GOVERNMENT CORPORATIONS WANT

Many of the most disgusting excesses of the current system are carried out by corporations/big business. Why, you may ask, overthrow the government? Why not get rid of corporations instead?

Let's look at the relationship between the U.S. government and the American- and foreign-based corporations that do business within our borders. The long-assumed link between democratization and free markets has been debunked by the economic rise of China, a totalitarian state that has morphed into authoritarianism yet registers impressive increases in GDP. Meanwhile, the post-2008 economic crisis has hit the Western liberal democracies the hardest.

The real link is between corporations and government, and it goes in only one direction.

The U.S. government can easily exist without corporations. There are, after all, dozens of alternate ways to organize a business: sole proprietorships, joint ventures, partnerships, and so on. But corporations cannot do business without a government. Corporations require a state for its police, armies, diplomats, and other officials to beat down uppity workers, to defend their centers of operation, and to expand global markets and resource grabs. Consider "failed states," where the lack of a strong central government creates political instability: violence, theft, and corruption, not to mention the businessperson's bitterest foe, unpredictability. Because failed states don't provide law and order, courts to enforce contracts or stable currencies, they can't attract foreign or domestic investment.

Each year *Foreign Policy* magazine publishes its Failed States Index. The most recent year available at this writing, 2009, leads with a list of countries where essential services have largely ceased to be delivered to the population. They also read like a top-ten list of nations where no sane businessperson would ever consider setting up a business concern: Somalia, Zimbabwe, Sudan, Chad, Congo, Iraq, Afghanistan, the Central African Republic, Guinea, and Pakistan. (The United States is ranked in the "moderate" category of viability, behind nineteen other countries, most of which are classified as "sustainable." The weakest points for the U.S., according to the magazine: "uneven economic development along group lines" and "suspension or arbitrary application of the rule of law and widespread violation of human rights."[91] But let's not digress further.) Granted, failed states suffer dire poverty, disease, low life expectancy, and all manner of hardship. But they do have one thing going for them: rapacious corporations can't establish a foothold.

In order for corporations to thrive, they need to operate within the borders of a government strong enough to control its frontiers, police its streets, maintain a judiciary, and do all the other things that citizens of modern nation-states expect: build and maintain transportation and communications infrastructure, educate workers, and so on. But businesses *prefer* a government that is not only merely amenable to their existence, but deferential to their concerns.

The 2004 Canadian documentary film *The Corporation* posits that the modern corporate structure that began in 1712—a group of businesspeople whose sole responsibility is fiduciary and who are protected from judicial accountability for their actions—is inherently antisocial, destructive, and in short, psychotic. The film ends with our friend Michael Moore marveling aloud about the fact that his films are distributed by major corporations: "[Corporations] believe that when people watch my stuff . . . they won't do anything, because we've done such a good job of numbing their minds and dumbing them down, you know, they'll never affect anything, people aren't going to leave the couch and go and do something political. They're convinced of that. I'm convinced of the opposite. I'm convinced that a few people are going to leave this movie theater or get up off the couch and go and do something, anything, and get this world back in our hands."[92]

Maybe they will—but not because of Moore's movie.

The danger presented by corporations is hardly new; there are more examples available to the critic of corporate-government collusion than paper to print them on. But few cases better symbolize the viciousness of the arrangement than the case of *Kelo v. City of New London*.

Prior to *Kelo*, municipalities had commonly used the legal doctrine of "eminent domain," the inherent power of the state to condemn and seize private property to serve a greater public good. A strip of a homeowner's land can be taken to allow the widening of a road; a farmer's field may have to make way for a railroad or pipeline. Governments are expected to pay fair market value in exchange for such expropriation. In 2005 the U.S. Supreme Court ruled that the city of New London, Connecticut, had the right to seize and evict homeowners and other real estate owners in the Fort Trumbell neighborhood to make way for a novel form of "public use": a private redevelopment project.

The New London scheme was co-sponsored by the city (which kicked in eighty million in tax dollars to buy land, demolish the homes, and fight the case) and the Pfizer pharmaceutical corporation. After the decision, a ninety-acre area was razed to make way for a 270-million-dollar conference center as well as a complex of luxury business hotels and condominiums. City officials acknowledged that the evictions were painful, but argued that a greater good would result: jobs and the redevelopment of what they portrayed as a blighted neighborhood.

Community activists fought the plan. They thought it was wrong and fiscally unsustainable. "The evidence at trial showed that nothing would be built on that land," said Dana Berliner, a lawyer for the homeowners. "The developer (who has now left the project) did a study showing there was no market for the biotech office buildings the city claimed would replace the homes. But the courts didn't want to look at that evidence."[93]

They were right. In late 2009 Pfizer announced that it was shuttering the few office buildings it had built in New London. Instead of creating new jobs, it laid off nearly fifteen hundred workers. "Now the homes are gone," wrote Paul Bass of the *New Haven Independent*, "and vast acres remain abandoned." Surprise, surprise. Cities from Portland, Oregon, to Portland, Maine, are pockmarked with vacant lots marking the sites where real estate developers tore down houses but ran out of cash before they could put up new ones. By the way, the Pfizer scoundrels walked away with millions in tax breaks.

As long as corporations exist, they will corrupt the governments of the countries in which they operate. Tibor Machan, a pro-capitalist conservative columnist, unwittingly concedes as much by trying to argue against it: "Is this some kind of pie in the sky aspiration, to have a system in which it is illegitimate for business and government to get into bed together? Well, it would appear to be difficult, of course, since corporations do have the resources to seek out government favors—although so do some other institutions, such as unions and universities. But just because they can, it doesn't follow that they have to and will. Quite possibly laws and public policy can be established that make the ties between business and government illegal."[94]

"Quite possibly."

Uh-huh. Call us when the shuttle lands.

I won't insult your intelligence by dwelling on this point. It's plainly obvious that no government corrupted by corporate campaign contributions and other forms of systemic and unofficial graft will ever pass, much less enforce, a law prohibiting government-corporate collusion. Since that is the case here and now, the solution is not to lobby the government to get rid of or control big business. It is to get rid of this government. Stable government is the water in which the big sharks of predatory capitalism swim.

WE AREN'T THE WORLD

Traditionally, leftists, especially communists, have posited the necessity of an international component in order to effect revolutionary change. Revolutionary struggles in Nepal, in India, and in Canada can help ignite the desire of Americans to liberate themselves. No doubt, an international uprising would stand a better chance of success than a U.S.-centric one; as the leaders of revolutionary France, Cuba, or Russia could attest, a revolutionary nation that stands alone becomes an island vulnerable to economic and military attack. Trade embargoes, devastating in the past, would be all the more so in our increasingly globally integrated economy. In 1968, revolutionary movements in the United States drew strength from and inspired those in Japan, Germany, Italy, Senegal, Brazil, and many other countries.

Uprisings overseas would and will set examples for us to follow. Americans will be inspired; when we act, we will inspire others. But we don't need people in other countries to act first.

Our situation is unique. As citizens and residents of the sole remaining superpower, one that even in our present dire circumstances remains an economic and military behemoth (with even the emerging Chinese colossus a distant second), we Americans can lead the way toward global rebellion. First and foremost, an American revolution would stand as an example too big to ignore. If we move first, people in other countries suffering similar or analogous circumstances will be influenced by our actions. Soon they will contribute to ours.

A revolt here would instantly liberate hundreds of millions of people in other countries—those occupied by American troops, subjugated by American-backed dictatorial and authoritarian regimes, and robbed by corrupt puppet rulers. These U.S. client states and satellites are reviled by the broad majority of their citizens. Most already have viable indigenous resistance movements waiting for their chance to seize power. The United States is the world's largest arms dealer, "ranked first for worldwide arms sales and it's fast expanding its lead," reported *Wired* magazine in 2009.[95] It supplies developing nations with 70 percent of all weapons sales. Thanks to an expansionist policy that maintains more than half a million men under arms and another half million employed as mercenaries around the globe, U.S. military expenditures amount to 41.5 percent of the world's total. (China, at 5.8 percent, is a distant second.)

Cut off those shipments and bring home our soldiers. The world will quickly become more peaceful.

The top two recipients of U.S. foreign assistance are Israel and Egypt. Were we to cut off the four billion dollars a year each currently receives in foreign aid (weapons and bribes), both the apartheid state of Israel and the Egyptian dictatorship of Hosni Mubarak would probably not be long for this world. Other countries where the loss of U.S. economic and military support for unpopular governments could lead to internally inspired regime change include Pakistan, Colombia, Peru, Sudan, Nigeria, and Uzbekistan. Certainly it would and should be possible for revolutionary movements in other countries to make common cause with Americans.

COLLAPSE? WHAT COMES NEXT?

Right now, of course, revolution seems improbable—perhaps even impossible. But the truth is we are currently in the run-up to the post-American era. What will it look like? Three questions will help us shape the answer.

First, when will the United States—in its current formulation—come to an end?

Most historians place the collapse of the Roman Empire at 476 CE, when the Visigoths sacked Rome. But Rome had been sacked by barbarian tribes before. Julius Nepos, the Western Roman emperor recognized by the Eastern Empire based in Constantinople, continued to rule until 480, when he was assassinated. The Ostrogoths took over. But they considered themselves successors, not replacements. The Senate remained in session; new emperors continued to claim dominion over the old (Western) Roman Empire for hundreds of years.

On the other hand, most people today agree that the

Soviet Union ended on Christmas Day 1991. But Soviet government entities continued to convene and issue rulings in the "former" Soviet republics as late as the mid-1990s. "Soviet" troop units remain in Soviet uniform and follow Soviet laws along the border between Tajikistan and Afghanistan. Turkmen citizens were still receiving new "Soviet" passports as of 2002. And millions of citizens of the former Soviet republics wish to see the USSR reconstituted. Is the Soviet Union dead? Or merely suffering through a temporary downturn? As Zhou Enlai famously told Henry Kissinger when asked his opinion of the French Revolution, "It is too early to tell." Unlike the Beatles, the Soviet Union could get back together any time.

What is certain is that every regime eventually comes to an end, that every empire collapses. For the simple reason that there are no exceptions, the United States of America will not be the first empire without an expiration date.

The second question is: How will the U.S. come to an end?

Will it collapse? Will there be a revolution?

In a collapse scenario, the old order ends without a new one ready to replace it. As happened in the former Soviet Union, there would be a tendency toward geographic disintegration. States, blocs of states, or culturally or geographically distinct regions within or across states will split off into independent republics or other forms of government. The dissolution of the American empire may cause boundary disputes and fractures; the post-Soviet era resulted in such cartographic weirdness as the de facto Nagorno-Karabakh autonomous enclave surrounded by Azerbaijan and a Trans-Dniester "frozen conflict" zone between Moldova and Ukraine, which still flies the Soviet flag. In a post-American situation distant territories and possessions like Guam and American Samoa would almost certainly lose contact with whatever remains of the old central government based in Washington. Hawaii, Alaska, even Texas and California might break away.

Economic collapse would hit some parts of the former United States harder than others. But, as we saw in Russia and the other fourteen former Soviet republics during the 1990s, most of the ex-U.S. would suffer high unemployment, declining wages, and in the hardest-hit areas, hunger. (Two million Russians starved to death during the 1990s.) If the situation looks anything like Russia after the Soviet collapse, it won't be pretty. "Russia's economy has shrunk almost every year," reported the *Economist* in 2000. "Output has fallen by about fifty-three percent in ten years, according to official (and notoriously dodgy) statistics . . . The physical infrastructure is decaying: hospitals, roads, prisons, schools and railways, with the exception of a few prestige projects in Moscow . . . are in a shamefully bad state. Russians are badly fed, badly dressed, badly housed, badly treated. The clearest sign of decay is that Russians die young and have so few babies.

The population is now smaller by six million people than it was a decade ago."[96]

In the former USSR, the vacuum of power was filled by the only social organization waiting in the wings during the late communist period: criminal gangs. Here in the United States, a disorganized dissolution of the existing system would likely devolve to a power grab by a right-wing coalition of Christian and assorted yahoos like the anti-immigrant vigilante group the Minutemen to survivalists to more mainline armed conservatives—think the National Rifle Association on speed. Criminal gangs old and new would grow in strength, especially in the cities.

The third question is: Why the U.S.?

We're responsible for more war, corruption, and brutalization of the planet than any other force in human history. Thus it behooves us not only to clean up our own mess, but to do so without pressuring other countries to follow our lead. Let other nations be responsible for themselves. Perhaps we will, for the first time in memory, begin to lead by example.

To sum up, the current crisis of confidence presents defenders of the status quo with the nearly insurmountable challenges characteristic of national decline. To future revolutionaries, the following are opportunities:

▶ Anger and despair are growing.
▶ Blame for the situation is rightly focused on corporations and the government that supports them.

▶ The current regime has been exposed as ineffectual and unresponsive to the people's most pressing needs.
▶ The current regime no longer seems invincible.

We are, in other words, in a revolutionary moment.

In 1915 Lenin declared that then, as in 1905, the Russian Empire was in a revolutionary crisis. "History seems to be repeating itself," he wrote. "Again there is a war. Again there is military defeat, and a revolutionary crisis accelerated by it. Again the liberal bourgeoisie . . . are advocating a programme of reform."[97] The 1905 Russian Revolution failed and Lenin fled into exile. But that's how it goes with revolutionary crises: the outcome isn't guaranteed. It merely opens the space for opportunity. The failed 1905 revolution led to 1917.

Our current situation contains some interesting parallels with what Lenin described.

First, the United States has suffered military defeat. And not just one, but a whole half-century plus of clusterfuckery! Since 1945 every major military conflict has ended in either a draw or a loss: Korea (loss), Vietnam (loss, with a generous helping of total humiliation), and the Gulf War (draw). Afghanistan and Iraq appear to be headed into the decisive loss category, although some optimists hold out for a draw in Iraq. Whatever. The United States has spent twenty-two trillion dollars on the military since the end of

World War II, and what does it have to show for it? Junk-yards filled with rusted artillery shells and madrassas full of young Muslims who wish we were all dead.

War isn't new to Americans. Nor is defeat. What *is* new is the public's realization and awareness of defeat *while it is happening.* Even as the Obama administration stubbornly ramps up its predecessor's occupation of Afghanistan, the majority of the voting public has turned against it. They don't think it's worthwhile, they don't think we can win, and they think the whole project was a mistake from the get-go. That's new. That's part of the fixings for a revolutionary crisis.

The other parallel certainly applies: the obsession with reform. Though talk of reform always abounds in American politics—the Right likes tax reform, that is, tax cuts, and the Left likes healthcare reform, that is, tax increases—the beginning of the Obama era saw a sharp spike in the rhetoric of reform.

In the 1970s, the moment of revolutionary crisis passed. The organized Left was exhausted. Mainline liberals, energized by the youth movement, grew older, graduated from college, and became careerists. Radicals were murdered, jailed, or marginalized. The same phenomenon came to bear as when a sports team is stuck in a losing streak: people get tired of not winning. In addition, mild reforms gave minor concessions to, or changed the conditions of, some categories among black people and women. A black middle class was given room to grow.

Now, at the beginning of another such moment, there is still time to mobilize people to act. Before we can spur people to action, however, we must bring them to understand what is going on. The situation is obvious to some of us. Our goal must be to raise the level of understanding more widely:

▶ Runaway, barely regulated free-market capitalism is at odds with the average person's right to be happy, healthy, and safe.

▶ Violent, constantly expanding militarism, the centerpiece of American foreign policy for over a century, drains the resources and energy we need to maintain and improve our own lives.

▶ The United States government, being composed as governments are everywhere of human beings who cling to power, cannot be reformed from within. Positive change can only be forced upon it.

▶ America's two-party system will never represent the vast majority of Americans, much less achieve national consensus.

▶ The United States' rhetorical claims to exceptionalism—of being "a shining city on a hill"—were always, well, unexceptional. Mourn not the passing of the United States when it comes. The ghosts of Native Americans, black slaves, and more recently, the people of Afghanistan and Pakistan will cheer. So should we, for their sake as well as our own.

▶ The system is in imminent danger of collapsing of its own accord. Unless people of good will work to create a new, better system and way of life to replace it, greedy, violent, and stupid people—religious extremists, racists, militarists—will. Doing nothing is not an option.

▶ This economic system is causing the utter depletion of resources upon which we all depend, plus the toxification and destruction of the environment, leading to the mass death of humans at least and the possibility of a dead planet at worst.

▶ There is the risk that what comes next could be worse. The Terror followed the French Revolution. Stalin's purges followed the Russian Revolution. Mass famine and the Cultural Revolution followed Mao's Chinese Revolution. We must take that chance. To do nothing is to concede defeat without a fight.

IV. NO ONE SAID IT WOULD BE EASY

1848: Publication date of "The Communist Manifesto"
1917: Beginning of the Russian Revolution
Elapsed Time: Sixty-nine years

Why, if Americans have never risen up en masse to over-throw a system most of them hate, will they do it now? I am tempted to respond: Because it's different this time. The economic situation is worse, the government is weaker, and people will soon be angrier and more desperate than at any time since the nineteenth century. All of which is true, but there's a better answer: the fact that they didn't do it before doesn't mean that they couldn't. That a bird chooses to sit on a branch doesn't mean that it can't fly. Revolution could have come to America in the 1920s, 1930s, and 1960s. It almost did. This revolutionary moment may pass; if it does and you are reading this years from now after the American capitalist-corporatist system manages to right itself and reassert its control, that merely means that the people missed another chance.

This book is not a prediction of what *will* happen. It calls attention to what *can* happen, if we make it happen, and why it can happen now.

The time, as Ronald Reagan's campaign slogan read, is now. If not now, when?

Everywhere you look, you see hopelessness. Homeless people with nowhere to go and no one to give a damn. Young people with no prospects of paying off their student loans or finding a job. Sick people with no way to pay for the care they need. Middle-aged men and women who should be enjoying the peaks of their careers "downsized," with no prospect of any job short of a menial, humiliating position at a discount retail outlet.

On a macro scale, hopelessness has permeated the system itself. Pundits call the 2000s "the Lost Decade." The stock market made no gains. Average living standards fell. Nothing was gained. The system failed.

Even when the same political party controls all three branches of government, it is stymied by gridlock. It can't accomplish anything significant. Investors despair for the economic future. There are no new revolutionary products or innovations waiting in the wings to stimulate optimism and investment. The government is out of energy and out of cash, flailing because there's no one and nothing with income left to tax and no creditors willing or able to finance new debt. The social safety net that ensures political stability is stretched, breaking and incapable of being fixed.

All around we see the psychic damage and floundering wreaked by the weaknesses of the political and economic reality of the United States and the Western world at the start of the twenty-first century: alienation, workplace and school shootings, a sharp spike in murder-suicides, excessive medication. Craziness all around.

The American people cherish the idea that they are better than everyone else, both as a country and as individuals. That they matter more than anyone else. That they deserve the best, not just the best that is their share, but everybody else's share, too. And that, perversely, this religion, the Cult of the Asshole, requires that we each sacrifice for the greater bad, that we must watch our children die untreated for disease and suck up pollution and allow government officials to torture and then not hold them to account—and why? Because everyone's right to happiness relies on a few people's right to bully and abuse and steal and vandalize everything and everyone so that *they* can be as happy as it is possible for anyone to be.

Six in ten believe that "enhanced interrogation techniques," including waterboarding, are a form of torture. But half the public approves the use of those techniques.
—CNN, 2009[98]

Hey, there has to be a dream.

But that crazy dream is dying. The trailer park patriot, his low-rent hovel festooned with Old Glory, is damned close to realizing that he will never win the lottery. Paying the rent at the trailer park is tough. So maybe he shouldn't worry about the maximum tax rate being raised.

The gung-ho soldier, still walking on two legs but minus a lot of faith in the country he once thought was good, is back from Somalia or Afghanistan or Iraq with a brand new, more realistic attitude.

The corporate stooge who neglected his wife and kids to work long hours, only to get laid off, finally gets it. He wasn't powerful merely because he wore a suit to the office.

The anesthetizing effect of television, sports, and video games is wearing off. Hopelessness is upon us. Anger comes next. Then rage. Let us hope—no, let's work to make sure—that that rage is directed where it belongs.

There are signs of readiness for change. When the latest round of the mass firings (don't call them "layoffs"; those are temporary) that have defined the working experience in the United States in recent memory began a few years ago, corporate employers found that workers were beginning to act collectively.

According to a 2009 study by the outplacement firm Challenger, Gray & Christmas, the most common budget-cutting methods employed by firms in the 2008-to-whenever depression were hiring freezes and slashing travel budgets.[99] This is a big change from previous cyclical downturns, when companies favored mass firings. Burned by high turnover and low morale following those experiences, managers often ask workers what kind of pain they prefer. More often than not, they're accepting pay cuts and furloughs rather than see their colleagues lose their jobs.

The Reagan revolution, which threw out the traditional social contract in favor of the dubious argument that society benefits overall when individuals act selfishly, is dead. Americans are starting to come to the same conclusion citizens in the post-Soviet republics reached after the demise of the USSR: inequality of income and wealth is sick. Having traveled throughout what used to be the Soviet Union over the course of more than a decade, I have heard countless people tell me that they missed the old system. No one articulated their thoughts better than Kamal, an ethnic Russian living in Dushanbe, the capital of Tajikistan. By Tajik standards, Kamal is successful: a driver and tour guide, he freelances for local travel agencies and owns his own car, a Mitsubishi Montero. "In Soviet times I dreamed of owning all the things that Westerners had: jeans, records, leather jacket, my own car," he told me as we banged up the Bartang River valley in southern Tajikistan near the Afghan border. "And now I have those things and more. I am doing a lot better under capitalism than I was in Soviet times." But, if he had the choice, he'd go back in a second. "I can't enjoy myself knowing that so many other people are doing worse. Before, we were all the same. We didn't have much, but we had enough. It was better." It's easier to sink or swim together than going it alone.

Militarism, the "America: Love It or Leave It" mentality that has long served as one of the basic underpinnings of the system's means of self-protection, is fading. Yes, a sour economy always prompts people to push to have more resources directed domestically, to take care of "America first." But it's different this time. To a degree that's even more pronounced than the malaise that followed the U.S. defeat in Vietnam, the disastrous wars in Afghanistan and Iraq have forced us to see that our country can no longer conquer and win and exploit without end. Of course, it has been many decades since we "won" a war. But now we're starting to realize it. Like Great Britain post-India and France after Indo-China and Algeria, we see that empire has its limits.

To paraphrase a line from the Bush years, a revolution now would be the right war at the right time. It's necessary to stave off the horrors of uncontrolled political collapse. For people who care about making life better for themselves, for other people, and for other living things, it's a moral imperative. And a material one—we can't live without a healthy planet. And let's face it—we're not likely to see the stars align like this for a long time. Americans are furious and desperate and rapidly becoming more of both. A people notable for their passivity—home of the brave, my ass!—just might be ready to get off their asses and stand up for themselves and for what's right.

The system is weak. Exhausted. Nearly dead of its own accord.

It's time.

BEATING A STATE WITHOUT OPPOSITION

It won't be easy.

The United States government is the most efficient fascist state ever created—even more ruthless and effective than Nazi Germany. Think that's an exaggeration? Consider the most obvious point: *It has no internal opposition.*

None.

Officially sanctioned and internally tolerated "loyal opposition" groups don't count. There's a reason that, in authoritarian states elsewhere, journalists are bound with duct tape and chucked out the windows of tall buildings, that opposition politicians disappear, never to be seen again, that pulling out a protest sign in front of a public building can earn you a long, brutal stretch in prison. That reason is *not* that the U.S. is a freer place. On the contrary—the U.S. regime tolerates internal dissent *because it poses no threat to its existence or hold on power.*

The official Left, which is the Democratic Party and its liberal allies, and the official Right, which is the Republican Party and its conservative allies, validate the American system's self-advertised "moderation." They can say or do whatever they want—as long as they don't question the system *itself*.

Even Adolf Hitler had to contend with a number of serious internal challenges to his government. Anti-Nazi officers in the German high command repeatedly plotted to assassinate Hitler and overthrow the Nazi regime; on several occasions they came close to succeeding. Although there is political resistance on U.S. campuses to government policies, particularly those concerning foreign wars, few if any American college students actively call—as groups like the White Rose did against the Nazis—for replacing the current government with an entirely new form.

America's form of government, authoritarianism masquerading as liberal democracy, is actually more formidable a political adversary than a totalitarian state. We can see this clearly in post-Soviet Russia, where the authoritarian pseudo-democracy of Vladimir Putin cracks down with greater ferocity and efficiency on political dissidents than the Soviet state did. "While Soviet dissidents could strategize to protect themselves—knowing, for example, that prosecutors needed at least two witnesses— their tricks are of no use in a post-Soviet justice system, where cases can be wholly fabricated," said Lyudmila Alexeyeva, a famous eighty-two-year-old political dissident who goes up against the USSR as well as the independent Russian Federation, in the *New York Times*.[100]

"In a sense," said Tanya Lokshina of the Moscow office of Human Rights Watch, "it is easier, strategy-wise, to be opposed to a full totalitarian regime than it is to try to counter a more sophisticated, strongly authoritarian one. There is some freedom. How do you explain to people what exactly they are lacking?"

Heretofore one of the cleverest self-preservation tactics deployed by American authorities has been the co-opting of opposition. Of the two major political parties, one is by definition out of power at any given time. Yet the minority's opposition to the ruling majority party functions as a member of the "loyal opposition," in British parlance. In matters of high structural priority to the two-party duopoly—such as war—the minority party often votes unanimously (or nearly so) along with the majority. Only one member of Congress, Democrat Barbara Lee of California, voted against the 2001 invasion of Afghanistan. Similarly, the 1964 Gulf of Tonkin Resolution that marked the start of the Vietnam War passed unanimously.

Dozens of "third parties" manage to get placed on the ballot in various states. In recent years notable third-party presidential runs have included those of John Anderson in 1980 and Ross Perot in 1992. Currently, major third parties include the center-right Libertarian Party and the Green Party. But all third parties, even those whose ideology runs to the extreme right or extreme left, work within the narrow constraints of the system. This is true despite the fact that the two major parties have enacted laws and institutions, like the Electoral College with its winner-take-all system, that ensure that third parties can't gain traction or grow.

Third parties are marginalized in the press. Third-party candidates, openly ridiculed and turned away from debates (as the Green Party's Ralph Nader was in 2004), accomplish little save publicizing their next book. The existence of fringe parties, such as the right-wing America First Party, and even those that claim to adhere to Marxist-Leninist principles (the Socialist Workers Party and the Communist Party USA) actually help legitimize a system that censors them in the media, keeps them off the ballot, and ensures they will never be permitted to achieve power. "Dispels the myth that the CPUSA is or ever was a supporter of violent revolution," reads the title of a typical entry on the party's website—as though impotence was something to brag about.

Under the umbrella of officially tolerated politics, any whiff of rebellion is quickly stamped out. During the 2008 presidential race, Obama immediately threw his long-time pastor the Reverend Jeremiah Wright under the proverbial bus after it was revealed that Wright had called out the U.S. government for some of its (well-documented) sins. A strategist for Hillary Rodham Clinton's primary campaign named Geoffrey Garin was even attacked over a piece he wrote for a college newspaper at age twenty: "On this [1973] anniversary [of the Boston Tea Party] we must recognize that the patriots of Boston acted wisely in overthrowing their oppressors and the time is come to express our confidence in what our forefathers did by doing it ourselves."[101]

Third-party pseudo-alternatives serve several purposes. They release pressure and channel would-be opponents into harmless organizations. There they spin their wheels, attending meetings and bemoaning their lack of influence until they drop into their graves, brimming with idealism, dirt, and worms.

No American third party has ever directly or indirectly worked toward revolutionary overthrow of the government.

Minor parties get ignored during the elections, with the exception of the quadrennial "There Are Other Parties, You Know" story on broadcast news. You know how it goes: "You've already heard a lot from Dwight Eisenhower and Adlai Stevenson. Believe it or not, there are *other* candidates on the ballot too! Let's take a look at these so-called 'third party' candidates. The Libertarian Party, for example, is running in all fifty states. They say they're growing!" This is followed by the usual newsroom banter: "Wow, Mike, that sure was interesting. Are you going to vote for one of these other candidates?" "Don't be silly, Daphne! I like my vote to *count*. Now let's check in with Bob to see how the Yankees did last night."

When nonmajor party candidates succeed, they do so by embracing the official media's image of them as a media joke. The biggest independent success story in recent history was the victory of former professional wrestler Jesse "the Body" Ventura, who became governor of Minnesota in 1998 in spite of—or perhaps due to—his tenuous hold on the English language. To Ventura's credit, he studied up and tried to impose some meaningful reform concerning spending allocations. But he was unable to govern without allies in the state house, which was controlled by Democrats and Republicans.

Some will point to the media as a source of opposition to the regime and its basic principles. However, cursory consideration reveals that the Fourth Estate, from the big television networks down to the most insignificant individual blogger, uniformly supports the status quo, at least by tacit consent.

Facts that might bring discredit or dishonor upon the power elite, no matter how pertinent to a story, are routinely censored from the media. Accounts of tensions between the U.S. and "anti-American" Venezuelan president Hugo Chávez, as he is routinely referred to, inevitably omit the well-documented fact that the Central Intelligence Agency attempted to remove him via a coup d'état. This would, of course, put Chávez's antipathy toward the U.S. and its foreign policy in context. Similarly, stories of reporters murdered in Central Asia republics like Kyrgyzstan and Kazakhstan fail to mention that those governments are propped up with weapons and other U.S.

aid. Coverage of the January 2010 earthquake in Haiti described ex-president Jean-Bertrand Aristide's ins and outs of power but omitted mention of the CIA's intimate involvement in his fortunes.

Among existing organizations and personalities, the left-in-waiting—the academic radicals, leftie websites, people like, well, me—will hopefully find some way to make themselves useful to any effort to seize power so that we may take control of our lives. But it will almost certainly not be in the context of existing institutions. New groups, new ideas, and new political stars will and should rise to address the needs and concerns of the people as the revolution begins, matures, triumphs, and consolidates power.

As we discussed earlier, we Americans are not allowed to talk about actual opposition to the overall system. We cannot discuss our desire to get rid of everyone and everything we despise and replace them with people and things we prefer. We may ask politely for change. If our requests are refused, as such requests always are, we are expected to smile and walk away quietly, considering ourselves lucky to be allowed to live and breathe the sweet air of ersatz liberty despite our faithlessness and insolence.

Calling for reform is okay. Calling the system broken and in need of replacement is treason.

A person who seeks to seize power cannot count on the support of any existing party or political organization. As the scattered and confused Frenchmen and Frenchwomen who gathered to form the disparate cells that eventually formed the Resistance during World War II had to do, American revolutionaries will have to find like-minded comrades, friends they can trust with their lives one person at a time. They will form cells, networks, and "rhizomatic" political organizations that are, like weeds, intertwined, lateral, and connected to other groups. These groups and subgroups will eventually need to coalesce into some sort of partylike organization to take and wield state power—but first things first. Two people agreeing to trust one another with their lives is where it begins, in an oath where more is at stake than one concerning love or marriage.

Even among the most politically conscious Americans, change that doesn't rely on reform (which is by definition voluntary) is almost impossible to fathom as a realistic option. This is partly due to inertia—any government that has remained in power over two centuries seems immune to removal. It's partly due to the simple fact that the U.S. is such a behemoth: the world's sole remaining super-power, equipped with an awesome military-security state apparatus capable of obliterating enemies with the push of a button by remote control from thousands of miles away, its vast territory supplemented by an even vaster empire of colonies, territories, puppet and client states, not to mention vassal states cowed into economic and military neutrality. Regardless of whether one is thinking empirically or viscerally, the odds associated with confronting this colossus seem insurmountably long.

And scary.

I worry that writing these words could land me in prison. I worry that daring to mention the idea of revolutionary change, real change, the kind that can happen only outside the system, will ruin my career and destroy my livelihood. Sure, by this country's right-wing standards of what constitutes "mainstream," I am considered outspoken. Yet I have always worried, always pulled my punches about what should be done, betrayed myself and my fellow Americans by embracing cowardice. This is not to say that I was always a radical. Far from it. Like many commentators, my political journey has meandered all over the ideological landscape. I have worked for the Democratic Party, flirted with political organizations of various stripes, including libertarian, considered ideas from far left to far right. As recently as six years ago, I wrote a book titled *Wake Up! You're Liberal!* (In my defense, I hated the title. And I didn't say that *I* was a liberal—just that you are. Which is still probably true.) But I have concluded several times throughout my life that nothing short of the radical actions I call for in this manifesto would be sufficient to save us, our nation, and the world with its plants and animals—and I have been afraid to say so.

On the other hand, why should I fear what might happen? How dare I? I am asking people to take far greater risks than marginalization, imprisonment, or even death. I am asking them to recognize that their world, everything they love, everything they know, and everything they hate is coming to an end. I want them, rather than cling to the familiar as long as they can, like a passenger on a sinking ship climbing the mast to stave off cold reality, to instead take charge of their destiny and get rid of everything they love because it is also everything they hate. Death should not deter us: Everyone dies. Jail shouldn't be that scary: One out of three African-American men is in prison or on probation. Yet the number of truly independent-minded Americans willing and able to commit to what can and should and must be done at this time is a fraction of a fraction of a fraction of a percent.

These rare souls carry out acts of resistance on a freelance basis—members of "groups" that aren't organizations at all, but rather lists of principles and precepts posted on websites and distributed by email chain letter: the Earth Liberation Front and Animal Liberation Front, for example. As with the Islamist organization Al Qaeda, these concepts are transmitted virally, deliberately eschewing even the traditional three-man cell structure (each fighter recruits two more, and each person knows only the two people below him and the one above him in the chain of command) and turning the Internet against its makers by letting the ideas *be* the leaders. Radical environmentalists living in a community see what they think needs to be done (burn down environmentally unsustainable McMansions in a new development, torch SUVs in the lot of a car dealership, torch a ski lodge being built on the habitat of an endangered lynx) and do it. They adopt the ELF label and vanish into the night. Back to their jobs as barristas or whatever. Unless they're stupid enough to talk, no one is the wiser.

Freelance violence will always play an important role in attempts to overthrow a power structure. They can, as residents of Nazi-occupied Europe learned at the beginning of their ordeal, build up support by demonstrating that action is possible. Sometimes they can be a real pain in the ass; the 1999 Battle of Seattle, for instance, slowed the momentum of corporate globalization by throwing the World Trade Organization into chaos for years. And all it took was a few broken windows! By 2001 the Federal Bureau of Investigation had designated ELF as the number-one most dangerous terrorist organization in the world. (This was *after* Al Qaeda blew up two American embassies in East Africa in 1998 and bombed the USS *Cole* in 2000.)

But these slightly-more-than-symbolic acts are secondary at best. They can never prove decisive in the struggle. "The FBI estimates that the ALF/ELF have committed more than six hundred criminal acts in the United States since 1996, resulting in damages in excess of forty-three million dollars,"[102] the chief of the FBI's counterterrorism division testified to Congress in 2002. Sounds impressive. But the

United States spends more than one billion dollars a week just to occupy Iraq.

Gun sales surge after Obama's election
—CNN headline[103]

There is no real left—only loyal opposition—in the United States. But the Right is real and ready to rumble. There has been an explosion of armed militia groups tied to the "Patriot" movement, which overlaps with Tea Partiers. According to a 2010 report by the Southern Poverty Law Center, "Since the installation of Barack Obama, right-wing extremists have murdered six law enforcement officers. Racist skinheads and others have been arrested in alleged plots to assassinate the nation's first black president."[104] They are opening camps in rural areas, accumulating weapons and training new members in their use, and rallying their forces to engage in acts of intimidation (such as attending presidential rallies with automatic weapons and going to Starbucks with sidearms strapped to their legs).

More notably, media and political figures on the mainstream Right vocally legitimize these groups. After the Department of Homeland Security report about the rise of extremist rightists was released, a conservative caller told radio personality Rush Limbaugh that he "agreed" with it:

"Well, because, you know, we're the people that want to go back to the Constitution, that, you know, really love our freedom and understand that it's being taken away, and therefore we pose an enormous threat to the government. We're the people buying guns and storing ammunition and preparing for the time when we have to fight the government off."

Limbaugh's response: "Wait a minute, though. I understand the point you're trying to make, but that's not extremism."

Caller: "Well, to them it is."

Limbaugh: "But it's not. They don't get to define the terms. We are not extremists."[105]

There's nothing similar on the Left. There's no armed militia group. Even if there were, there would be no mainstream liberals with the reach of Rush Limbaugh willing to endorse it.

IT'S US OR THEM

Thomas Jefferson famously posited that revolution was a good thing, that he never expected nor wanted the American government he helped create to last forever. Yet it is against the law to promote the overthrow of the government. An even bigger paradox is the fact that, in the United States, violent revolution is promoted primarily by counterrevolutionary right-wingers. Searches for the phrase "violent revolution" online yield links to various rightist extremist organizations. Some are black-helicopter paranoids, others are anti-Semites who fret about "international bankers," and still others lament Barack Obama's presidency with racially tinged outrage. What many of them have in common is that they're preparing for the crunch: they exchange information about weapons, brag about their stockpiles, and discuss plans and current construction of training camps. They are preparing for war. Against whom? The federal government, mainly. But it isn't hard to read between their lines. Minorities, immigrants, gays, atheists, leftists, and anyone else who doesn't fit into their white, Christian, male-dominated vision of what constitutes "American values" would soon become targets.

One Matt Wayne, writing for a website called SodaHead, expresses the New Right's mélange of New Left rhetoric (against "fascism"), John Birch-style nativism, and post-9/11 worship of the military (in this case, I imagine, wildly misguided):

> I sincerely hope that we don't have a civil war in our country. Most Americans are civilized and realize that wars cause pain, death, misery and destruction. But I think the time is near when decent law abiding patriotic Americans will decide enough is enough and they will resort to revolution. Patriotic Americans love their country and

abide by the law of the land and our constitution.
But when the freedom and rights afforded them by
the constitution are threatened they will revolt. We
have seen peaceful demonstrations by senior citizens [presumably referring here to the Tea Party
protests] throughout the US. The peaceful demonstrators have been defamed, called un-American
and Nazis by Obama and the democratic leadership. I fear a violent revolution is imminent. When
the decent young Americans wake up to the fact
that the Obama change is depriving them of their
God given rights and destroying our country, they
will join hands with the once peaceful citizens, and
a bloody revolution will begin. Many believe it's not
too far in the future. The military commanders will
be reluctant to fire upon once decent peaceful citizens that are merely attempting to regain their
constitutional rights. Even orders by the Com-
mander in thief, Obama, will not be obeyed by
these patriotic Commanders.[106]

Some sample responses:

"I don't see Americans getting violent yet. If the racist
Obama gets re-elected there might be [violence]. How
much more will white America take?"

From someone who calls himself Johnny Death-
hammer: "We can only abide so much, our patience with

these rats is at an end, we are getting ready. Patriots versus traitors, law abiding citizens of the Republic against the criminal elements within our Government, and our cities. Let the call go out, ENOUGH!"

"You have no clue as to how much training these patriots have. Nor how well armed we are. I hope this is settled by elections. But to allow our system to be subverted by socialism while we do nothing is intolerable. If you won't be part of the bid for continued freedom, then you will be a liability."

Do not assume that these sentiments are limited to fringe militia types living in the middle of the woods in the upper peninsula of Michigan. "Mainstream" right-wing Republicans have been itching to seize power from what they perceive as a vast Jewish communist liberal cabal that has controlled the media and the government for many years. In 1933, for example, top officials of the American Legion, the military veterans organization, approached a popular retired general, Smedley Butler, and offered him the support of five hundred thousand armed veterans to forcibly install him as a so-called Secretary of General Affairs—a de facto dictator. FDR would have remained president, but as a figurehead. (Butler went to the press.)

More recently (September 2009), John Perry wrote a column for the widely read right-wing blog Newsmax where he called for replacing President Obama with a military junta: "Imagine," he wrote, "a bloodless coup to restore and defend the Constitution through an interim administration that would do the serious business of governing and defending the nation. Skilled, military-trained, nation-builders would replace accountability-challenged, radical-left commissars." Syndicated conservative talk radio host Michael Savage said around the same time:

> The white male in particular—the one without connections, the one without money—has nothing to lose, and you haven't seen him yet. You haven't seen him explode in this country, and he's still a majority, by the way. In case you don't know it. He is still the majority. No one speaks for him. Everyone craps on him. People use him for cannon fodder. And he has no voice whatsoever. He has nobody speaking for him. So he goes to these extreme fighting events. Take a look at them, and you'll see what the white male is capable of. And you're going to find out that if you keep pushing this country around, you'll find out that there's an ugly side to the white male that has been suppressed for probably thirty years right now, but it really has never gone away.

And during the 2000 Florida recount crisis, Bush's representatives went on PBS's *NewsHour with Jim Lehrer* to threaten violence should Al Gore be declared the winner of the election. "If we keep being put in the position of having to respond to recount after recount after recount of the same ballots," spat James Baker III, "then we just can't sit on our hands, and we will be forced to do what might be in our best personal interest—but not—it would not be in the best interest of our wonderful country. And what's happening now, if I may say so, is not in the best interest of our country. And there is a way to stop that. There's a way to bring this thing back before it spirals totally out of control."[107]

Not in a legal way, mind you.

In April 2009 the Department of Homeland Security issued an assessment warning that the hard right could soon become a threat to the U.S. government: "The DHS/Office of Intelligence and Analysis (I&A) has no specific information that domestic rightwing terrorists are currently planning acts of violence, but rightwing extremists may be gaining new recruits by playing on their fears about several emergent issues. The economic downturn and the election of the first African American president present unique drivers for rightwing radicalization and recruitment."[108]

Is the threat of a right-wing takeover real? I think so. I think it has been real for decades; racist and nativist extremism is closely interwoven in our national fabric. But of course it's impossible to know whether the far right can seize power.

Let's say, for the sake of argument, that the crunch is

coming. That a power vacuum is about to be created by the implosion of the existing economic and/or political systems. Which is the smarter course of action? Getting prepared to step into the breach? Or continue to passively sit on our asses, hoping things will improve by themselves?

Westerners like to look down on the political systems of Central Asia and sub-Saharan Africa, denigrating them as beholden to tribalism. Smug and superior, we imagine ourselves better off living in nations that don't have "tribal elders" or, as in Somalia, "clans." But the truth is it's no different here. In the final analysis, struggles for political power always come down to tribalism. Here, in the United States, it's about entrenched power, not family lineage. Who will run things? Who will tell whom what to do? Who will be in charge? Smart, committed, energetic people? Or inbred hicks? Those who work? Or those who exploit them?

"In the latest report on hate crime in 2006," reads the 2009 report from Human Rights First, "the FBI identified 7,722 incidents—a 7.8 percent rise from the documented 7,163 crimes in 2005. There was a 9.5 percent rise in hate crime victims, from 8,804 in 2005 to 9,642 in 2006" (only a sixth of the nation's police departments kept track of hate crimes in 2006).[109] If the perpetrators of this violence gain power, they will exploit (and sometimes, perhaps more regularly, murder) those they dislike.

V. KNOW YOUR ENEMY

*We are all judges, assessing constantly. Every living crea-
ture constantly appraises every fellow creature, every
sound and smell and soil condition (in the case of
Jerusalem crickets, say, or earthworms). Every living creature in the wild uses its every capacity to discern as keenly
as possible what is safe, what is edible and what they can
have sex with. This is the survival instinct. This is evolution at work. Living creatures were given the power to
judge and the purpose of that power is to make sure at
least some of us survive. But judgment is being bred out
of our own species. In school, at home, in the media—
carefully, deliberately [younger generations] are being told
that they don't have the right to appraise others based on
their private criteria.*

—*Psychology Today*, May 14, 2009[110]

The utter lack of government interest in punishing villains
and villainy appears to be something new. Consider *The
9/11 Commission Report*, which detailed criminal neglect or
worse in various government and corporate bodies, but
recommended no punishment or accountability of any
kind whatsoever. Or the top honchos of the Bush administration who authorized the kidnapping, torture, and

murder of thousands of people, including children. That the Obama administration expressed their disinclination to investigate, much less prosecute, them was to be expected. The relationship between the wealthy and their pet politicians is mutually beneficial. What was surprising was that, despite extensive media coverage and public outrage, nobody did anything.

There is evil in the world. It occurs when people choose to do wrong—especially when they do it for money, power, or just plain fun. And it runs rampant when society greets it with a shrug.

No, everyone is not doing their "best." No, it is not acceptable to go to business school. Or to join the military. Or to fire employees while paying yourself tens of millions of dollars a year. Or to underpay people. People must be held accountable. Obviously, punishment can go too far. The *épuration*, the settling of scores that followed the Nazi withdrawal from France at the end of World War II, led to the deaths of thousands of collaborators, as well as innocents who didn't get a fair trial in the heat of the moment. The excesses of the Cultural Revolution are well known. But the memory of those periods in French and Chinese history help keep people honest during nonrevolutionary times. There's a lot to be said for rocking it Old School. Americans' moral relativism (especially among liberals) has prevented accountability for far too long—and things have gone way too far in the opposite direction.

As Jean-Paul Sartre said, we are the sum total of our actions. What is in our hearts does not matter. What we do does. A person who successfully suppresses his murderous rages and commits acts of generosity is good. One who claims to have good intentions, yet never seems to deliver, is evil. Everyone has a choice, second after second, year after year. These decisions can be difficult. Sometimes you must agonize over what to do. But if there is more than one choice, then one of them—however bad—will be a better decision than the other(s).

The first step is to define evil. Then point to the people who do evil: the politicians, bureaucrats, corporate executives, media power brokers, and environmental exploiters who spend every waking minute thinking up new ways to fuck us over and rape the world we live in to make an extra buck.

Stop tolerating the intolerable.

VI. TACTICS FOR THE HERE AND NOW

A single nonrevolutionary weekend is infinitely bloodier than a month of total revolution.

—Situationist graffiti, Paris, May 1968

If nothing else, the Myers-Briggs Type Indicator test is a fun parlor game for a rainy day. How you answer a set of multiple-choice questions determines your assignment to one of sixteen distinct Jungian personality types. My friends and relatives have found it remarkably accurate. So have I.

According to Myers-Briggs, I am an INTJ, or "mastermind," personality. INTJs, which account for between 1 and 4 percent of the population, "apply (often ruthlessly) the criterion 'Does it work?' to everything from their own research efforts to the prevailing social norms. This in turn produces an unusual independence of mind, freeing the INTJ from the constraints of authority, convention, or sentiment for its own sake,"[III] wrote Marina Margaret Heiss. INTJs aren't impressed by degrees, honorifics, or fancy titles. If someone isn't working out, INTJs don't care if that person went to Harvard (as did George W. Bush and

Barack Obama). If a plan or system is broken, INTJs get rid of it.

The United States doesn't work anymore. Capitalism never worked well; now it's irredeemable. Our political and economic leadership not only makes consistently bad decisions—it knows its decisions are bad, yet makes them anyway. An example: on Christmas Day 2009 a young Nigerian man smuggled the components of a bomb onto a Northwest Airlines flight from Amsterdam to Detroit in an attempt to blow up the plane as it approached Detroit. As typically follows such incidents, the media and various political figures asked what security measures could be put in place to prevent a reoccurrence. One idea quickly emerged: requiring passengers to pass through full-body scanning machines. These machines show the outline of a person's body and anything they're carrying in their pockets or under their clothes—coins, cell phones, keys, and bombs. Privacy experts worry that airport security workers will get off on looking at people's body shapes as revealed by the high-tech scanners. But those concerns were dismissed after the Northwest bombing attempt. What went unspoken by thousands of talking heads were two obvious points: First, whatever thrill results from abstracted naked body scans is bound to fade after viewing the first ten thousand passengers. Second, the scanners won't work! Would-be terrorists study security precautions and work around them. In the future, similar bombs can and will be smuggled inside the rectum.

Seven months before the Detroit incident, security technologist Bruce Schneier said on CNN that whole-body imaging technology "works pretty well." But he thought investing in ever-increasing levels of tech-based security measures was a waste of money. "It's stupid to spend money so terrorists can change plans . . . There's a huge 'cover your ass' factor in politics, but unfortunately, it doesn't make us safer."[112]

Any society that invests millions in a program that everyone knows can't possibly work is broken. So is one that repeats the same mistakes the same way. "It's totally frustrating," said Tom Kean, former New Jersey governor and the chairman of the commission that investigated the September 11, 2001, attacks, after it turned out that the federal government had previously been made aware of the intentions of Umar Farouk Abdulmutallab, the young man accused of the Detroit attempt, yet had issued him a visa to travel to the United States. "It's almost like the words being used to describe what went wrong are exactly the same [as those used to describe how the government failed to prevent 9/11]."[113] Eleanor Hill, staff director of the congressional inquiry into 9/11, echoed Kean's sentiments: "There seems to have been the same failure to put the pieces of the puzzle together and get them to the right people in time,"[114] she said.

We know *what* we need to do. But how? One thing is for sure: Old revolutionary models, with their old vocabulary and often alien origins, are not and can never be 100 percent applicable to the state of our nation in our times. We're not even sure America as a nation-state can or should survive. Looking to cut and paste old ideologies—communism, socialism, anarchism, libertarianism, Ruby Ridge–style right-wing survivalism—into our near future is doomed to failure. Revolutionary goals will develop organically after revolution has begun, as those who seek to replace the failed state argue and fight and float ideas among themselves and the broader public at large.

If and when the crunch comes, any organized political party will be broken up, its leaders and allies arrested and possibly jailed, tortured, and/or executed. The police will be thorough. Any party or leader that is not broken up, co-opted, arrested, or forced underground, prima facie, obviously does not present a danger to the existing order. Otherwise he/she/they would not remain free. Whether they are agents of the state or merely ineffective, preexisting opposition groups and personalities operating above ground must logically be presumed to be part of the system whether actively or passively. They are of no use whatsoever to the resistance movement. We cannot count on existing structures.

For a time, especially during the initial period of unrest, there will be officially sanctioned and tolerated nonviolent resistance—marching in the streets, peaceful opposition groups, outspoken opponents raising their voices in the media. In the final analysis, however—and this will become painfully clear as the crisis escalates— all of these work within the system and therefore for it. Those who would truly fight will be tempted to participate within these structures, but they would be committing a serious error, a security breach that could later endanger their lives and those of their comrades: by participating in open, public demonstrations, they will have identified themselves to the authorities. Though most of these pacifist pseudo-resisters will not present an actual danger to the continuing rule of the existing state, they will nonetheless be among the first to be rounded up and imprisoned (or worse) when the time comes. The woman or man who plans to participate in actual, that is, violent and furtive, revolution in the future should have nothing to do with the "official opposition."

Ironically, the people most psychologically prepared to overthrow the state are militantly opposed to running one. Howard J. Ehrlich wrote in *Reinventing Anarchy* (1979): "Anarchy is not without leadership. It is without *followership* [emphasis Ehrlich's]. Leadership under anarchism . . . is exercised within an egalitarian framework: that is, it is based not on the presumption that the leader is a superior person but on the presumption that the leader knows more about the subject for which s/he is providing leadership . . .

Anarchist leaders attempt to influence outcomes through education, not through issuing directives."[115] Of course, this presumes that everyone is amenable to education and open to the truth if presented to them. How does one reason with the 55 percent of respondents to a 2004 CBS News poll who believe that man did not evolve, but was rather created by God?[116]

Radical anarchists understand the destructive, stupid, and vile nature of the existing system as well as the violent methods required to take it on, but oppose the inherent nature of organized nation-statehood—"statism" they and libertarians spit in unison—rather than the type of system and the kind of people running the U.S. Who knows? They may be right. What they fail to understand, however, is that it will always be impossible to convince everyone not to try to form a new nation-state. Once created, a power vacuum will be filled, whether by you or some asshole.

GIVE WAR A CHANCE

The would-be revolutionist faces an obstruction: pacifism. Although no meaningful political change has ever taken place without violence or the credible threat of violence, pacifism has been the state religion of the official Left since the end of the Vietnam War. Can it be a coincidence that progressives cannot point to a single significant political victory since the early 1970s?

During the last forty years, antiauthoritarians of all political stripes have eschewed violent tactics, limiting themselves exclusively to passive, nonviolent, and/or pacifist means of resisting the state. When I was in college at Columbia in the early 1980s, those of us who sought to pressure the university to divest itself of its investments in apartheid-era South Africa met to discuss what to do. Fairly early on, it was agreed by our steering committee to set our action at Hamilton Hall, an academic building that housed the dean's office of the main undergraduate school. However, a divide soon emerged. Most of the leaders wanted to chain the doors of the building and camp outside. Others, I among them, preferred to take a page from the militant student "strike" of 1968 and occupy the building. "It's January in New York City," I pointed out. "Not only will it do more to disrupt the university, it will be more comfortable." As usual, the pacifist faction won—mainly using the argument that we risked getting arrested for trespassing if we occupied the building. They camped outside and locked the doors instead. Of course, that still exposed them to legal action: locking the doors of a public building violates the fire code. The police were called to clear out the mini-tent city. Astonishingly, the police told the demonstrators what time they would show up. Anyone who didn't "want" to be arrested could leave beforehand. The protest leaders created a list of those who "wanted" to be arrested, along with their addresses and Social Security numbers, printed it out on a dot-matrix printer, and handed it to the cops when they arrived—in order to make their processing through central booking more efficient. *Wild in the Streets* it was not.

Building a radical insurgency will require participants to abandon the passive-pacifist mentality as well as to argue against it with others. Sweeping, comprehensive, in other words, radical change is only possible through violence or the proven willingness to use it. Consider, to choose examples at random, the decisions of the Palestinian Liberation Organization to work within the official Western-run "peace process" with Israel, and of the Irish Republican Army to disarm and end its campaign of terrorism against Great Britain. At this writing, it is obvious that violence got the PLO and IRA a lot farther than nonviolence. After using violence to achieve years of progress, the momentum toward an independent Palestinian state has stalled and the British occupation of Northern Ireland seems to be a fait accompli for the foreseeable future. As Peter Gelderloos wrote in *How Nonviolence Protects the State*: "Time and again, people struggling not for some token reform but for complete liberation—the reclamation of control over our own lives and the power to negotiate our own relationships with the people and the world around us—will find that nonviolence does not work, that we face a self-perpetuating power structure that is immune to appeals to conscience and strong enough to plow over the disobedient and uncooperative."[117]

The willingness to resort to violent means (as well as others) was effective in the Western world until the postwar era that began in 1945. Through the 1930s political demonstrations were always potential riots in the making. Major political parties in many Western countries partnered with associated paramilitary groups that engaged in street battles with rivals and even assassinated rival political leaders. In the United States unions used violence and the threat thereof to extract considerable concessions that resulted in significant improvements in wages and working conditions (sometimes as the result of their infiltration by organized criminal gangs).

The last hurrah of violent political opposition in the U.S. took place in the 1960s and early 1970s (the SLS, Black Panthers, Symbionese Liberation Army, Red Army Faction, FLN, Weathermen, and so on). Nonviolence became antiviolence, which devolved into a habit and eventually a cult. By the time Gelderloos published his book in 2007, he was able to write: "In my experience, most people who are becoming involved with radical movements have never heard good arguments, or even bad ones, against nonviolence." During this period, which began roughly around the 1970 Kent State shootings, no organized party or group has managed to effect real change. Wars of aggression have been waged on schedule. Rollbacks of social guarantees have proceeded apace. The vast majority of ordinary people have gotten clobbered economically. The rate of environmental degradation has accelerated.

This recent legacy will be difficult to overcome. We have become "sheeple": weak willed, cowardly, too concerned about our personal physical safety at the expense of the work that must be done and the risks that must be undertaken in order to accomplish it. As Al Qaeda's Maulana Inyadullah said after 9/11, "The Americans love Pepsi-Cola, we love death." Islamic martyrs, said Osama bin Laden in 1997, "love death as you [Americans] love life." That must change, not to fight Islamists (for that would be but a distraction), but to build the will necessary to take on the entrenched power structure. Everyone dies. It's only a question of when, how, and for what.

Of course, nonviolent protest can effect change. But not by itself. We must understand that, in these cases, neither the demonstrations themselves nor their nonviolent nature is what prompts leaders to modify their policies or behavior. It is only the credible threat of violence, the possibility that opposition could escalate to the next level, that makes "nonviolent" protest effective. You don't have to hit someone if they believe you will hit them. Therefore, after a revolution runs its course and "normalcy" returns to the streets, it will be possible for people to demand and obtain changes. We see this phenomenon in France, for example; the nation's rich history of revolution keeps the bourgeois technocratic leadership—even those on the political right—on its toes. No one wants to end up dragged out of the Élysée Palace in the middle of the night by an angry Parisian mob. In 2009 workers at a closed Renault-Peugeot automobile factory in France took over their former place of employment and threatened to blow it up—they piled up gas cylinders in plain sight—unless they received severance pay. Each worker received twelve thousand euros each. As parents learn when attempting to discipline their children, however, the threat of violence must be real. This necessitates the infliction of actual violence from time to time.

The major example of effective resistance against the U.S. and its postcolonial empire was carried out by foreigners on 9/11. Neither the U.S. nor the West caved in, but their (over)reaction served the purposes of the nineteen hijackers and those who prepared the plot with them. The invasions of Afghanistan and Iraq exposed the leaders of the American government as monsters, and radicalized moderate Muslims. It prompted the legitimization of torture, illegal detentions and kidnappings, and violations of cherished privacy and other civil rights that forced many American citizens to reconsider their longstanding assumption that their country was mainly a benevolent force in the world. Setting aside the basic immorality of murdering three thousand midlevel office workers, it was highly effective.

Some leftists think they can develop a revolution out of a mass movement. They plan protests that appeal to mainstream, less radical liberals, like marches against the war against Iraq, then hope to recruit militants from their ranks. In the long run, however, this tactic is counterproductive. Sure, asking people to show up and march is a way of polling/gauging popular opinion. But then recruits see nothing happen as a result. In the case of Iraq, the troops invade right on time. "Stop the Reagan budgets!" people scream. Yet nothing changes. "No bailouts for bankers!" they shout; again, nothing. People soon realize that (peaceful) mass protest is pointless, especially at a time when the system has become bolder and more reckless because it has been so long since its very existence was seriously challenged. In the final analysis, this realization serves to actually make the masses less potent and less angry, diverting their activist energies into bullshit. They give up, not because they don't care, but because it's a waste of time.

Still, despite everything, there is no better time than now.

First and foremost, because it *is* now. If not now, when? We are mortal. The system is broken. Our priorities are not being addressed. If things must change, things must change now. Not next week. Now.

Our time offers other advantages. Although eavesdropping technology has become increasingly sophisticated, the Internet offers the ability to centralize, organize, and market resistance and opposition to corners of the globe where the forward motion of history used to be imperceptible. Governments can turn off the Internet—we've seen that happen in China and Iran whenever the public gets rambunctious—but they also turn off their ability to monitor and track dissent. We can look to high-tech solutions employed by the new generation of underground organizations; for example, many radical Islamists carry "flash" drives of computer data that can be smashed if they are in danger of being arrested. They eschew cell phones and satellite phones. Notes are carried by hand or, better yet, memorized and transmitted verbally. Older methods of communication and propaganda, like printing pamphlets and brochures cranked out at private workspaces, may make a comeback since such workspaces are much more difficult to detect than websites.

We must educate people about what's wrong and teach them how to think so that they—*they*—can come up with solutions. As Marxists would put it, propaganda comes first. But the ability to absorb it intelligently is required before propaganda can be effective. Unfortunately, we don't have much time. We can't let another innocent man die in prison or another child fall prey to a disease because of lack of healthcare. Building the revolution must happen quickly.

They can wait until people have been taught how to recognize the truth when they see it, and then how to act.

Or—taking the viewpoint that says they've waited long enough—they can rise up now, with the people we/they already have, the segment of the population that already "gets it." Personally, I'd rather have twenty-five thousand committed revolutionaries willing to fight and die than five million dilettantes willing to march in the streets for a few hours on a sunny Sunday afternoon. But I'd rather not choose. I'd rather have both!

Of course, it's not up to me. It's up to us.

It's time to prepare. The Right is already armed. Now, while guns are legal and easily obtainable, is a good time for intelligent Americans to get them and learn how to use them.

Then again, maybe it's time to make common cause with the people we're most afraid of.

WORK WITH EVERYONE AND ANYONE

The enemy of your enemy is your friend (at least until you've defeated your enemy). That has always been true. The French Resistance during World War II comprised factions and political parties that had nothing in common. Indeed, they hated each other. Most were communists. But there were also right-wing Gaullists, even monarchists. Cells sprang up all over, all with different styles of leadership. Some were led by charismatic warlords; others were more democratic.

The disparate factions of the resistance in Nazi-occupied France learned to put aside their differences. They worked together, or at least stayed out of one another's way. Because they understood that defeating the Germans was their top priority, they formed an alliance of convenience. After D-Day, of course, they vied against each other for power. But they fought side by side when it mattered.

The French Resistance is notable as a quintessential example of a highly decentralized organization. Anyone who wanted to form a resistance cell could find a few friends and do so. Any set of cells could join to form a group. There was a nominal leadership based in London, the Free French led by General Charles de Gaulle, but mostly that was for show, to raise money from the Allies. Local resistance groups weren't asked to conform their politics to de Gaulle's representatives, who parachuted into France, visiting various groups with an offer none of them turned down: We'll send you weapons and money. All you have to do is fight the Germans—and fight them harder when we give the signal that troops are about to invade Normandy.

As the Afghan fighter Ahmed Shah Massoud is said to have toasted his fellow anti-Soviet *mujahedeen* during the 1980s, "First we kill the Russians. Next we kill each other." Sure, there will be disputes between factions about where to take the country next. But that civil conflict is for later, after victory—otherwise, there will be no victory.

The power and prevalence of high-tech espionage equipment and infiltration has led the most effective antigovernment organizations to do something even more radical than their aims. They have decentralized so radically that they have no leadership at all, or at most one who serves as an ideological inspiration. No one gives orders. There are no membership rites or initiations. They have an idea, not a plan. Anyone can "join" such a decentralized group. They simply decide that they agree with its aims, get together with some friends, and carry out an action that they decide furthers their ideology. And they drive governments crazy.

When "leaders" of such groups are arrested or killed, they become martyrs, more effective than ever as recruiters. If governments resort to heavy-handed police or military actions, they radicalize moderates and fence-sitters. The harder they fight, the faster they lose. (In France during the war, German reprisals were the most effective recruiting tool the Resistance could ask for.) What government officials don't realize is that the followers *are* the leaders. Sometimes local cells of nongroup groups like the Earth Liberation Front, Animal Liberation Front, and Al Qaeda carry out acts that other members—even early "leaders" and theorists—disapprove of personally. But they never disavow them. To the contrary: they either endorse them or remain silent. Anyway, the mere fact that self-appointed members of ELF—which is basically a set of principles posted on some websites anyone can find using Google—has carried out an action means that it is acceptable. The people decide.

A powerful idea can only be destroyed one way—by acquiescing to the demand it represents. Want animal rights activists to stop breaking into laboratories and vandalizing scientists' homes? Stop animal experimentation. As long as people care about an issue, the attacks will continue.

The most effective organization is no organization. These days, every radical political action—in other words, anything of consequence—is carried out by some nonorganization organization. They're the only ones who can avoid detection. Only they become stronger as state repression escalates.

The rise of the totally decentralized political movement dovetails with the death of the party system. Liberal Democrats are peeling off into nonparty issue-specific organizations and old-fashioned depoliticization. Conservative Republicans are splitting into factions like the Tea Party. Fewer Americans than ever identify themselves with either major party.

Parties are dead. They are hierarchical, stagnant, unimaginative, inflexible. Think of a fist clenching sand.

The harder they try to hold on to power and to popular support, the faster it slips out of their grasp.

Factions are wrong. They separate people who have more in common than not. They separate would-be revolutionaries along lines both real and arbitrary, but neither matter until the twin evil of government and big business has been smashed.

Ideology is stupid. For those of us who have no power, it doesn't matter what we would do if we did. We don't. Seizing power, taking out the idiotic, incompetent, greedy, evil, and stupid people who are ruining our lives is what matters.

We can only be strong—and decentralized—if we reach out to anyone and everyone who is willing to take on the existing system. If racist skinheads in Idaho have guns and training and resolve, straight-edge anarchist punks from Brooklyn should be willing to cooperate with them . . . or at least leave them be. Work with anyone. With luck there will time to split ideological hairs—but only after victory.

It is better to do nothing than to stage a half-assed revolt. Hopelessness is better than false hope, because as discussed above, apparent hopelessness feeds the rage needed to launch a mass uprising. Don't mobilize until you're actually ready to strike.

Gather as many allies as possible. Welcome anyone who wants to act. Don't lead. Get out of the way. But hurry.

We must get ready (yesterday).

VII. IT'S UP TO YOU

So long as the Revolution has not occurred, within the national framework and in a period of imperialist capitalism [the oppressed person] cannot will the ruin of the boss without willing his own as well.

—Jean-Paul Sartre, *Notebooks for an Ethics*[118]

Everywhere we turn, we find organizations. We have groups, theories, websites, meetings, and newsletters up the ass! We lack what we need most: action.

We must rid ourselves of our shitty, worthless, incompetent, evil-doing, planet-murdering government and its corporate and media allies.

We must step into the breach before the current system collapses; if we fail, even worse forces will replace them (and they will be more difficult to dislodge).

Before we can act, however, we must become angry. As the saying goes, if you're not angry, then you're not paying attention. Getting people to pay attention to what is happening to them, who is doing it to them, and why is the duty of everyone with a political pulse. They—you—must work on this every waking minute of every day. Your friends, family, and people willing to listen to you need you to help them see that the current state of affairs need not continue and that it's up to them to save themselves.

Next, we need to stop turning our anger into ourselves or against one another, while gobbling pills to keep sane. We need to direct that anger against its source: the people and institutions that are enslaving us.

No one can enslave you without your consent. We are our own wardens. We can leave our prison any time.

We must try. Even if we fail. Some Americans look down on the French because they were defeated by Germany in six weeks. Some don't know that ninety thousand French soldiers died losing the six-week Battle of France. Two hundred thousand more were wounded. Good does not necessarily prevail. There is shame only in not fighting.

Sixteen decades of industrialization separate us from the "nothing to lose but their chains" proletarians of 1848. We have much to lose: our comfortable homes, even our lives. But if we do nothing, we will lose without having fought.

Who among us wants to lose everything we most believe, everything we most love without even having fought to save those things? Who is willing to accept that we can't fix what's broken or that we can't dream of a better life—not only for future generations, but also for ourselves?

Fighting will be the hardest thing you have ever done. But—unless you choose to lay down and die—there is no other choice.

You won't be alone. I'll be there, and so will millions of others.

NOTES

1. Sarah Anderson and John Cavanagh, "Top 200: The Rise of Global Corporate Power," *Corporate Watch*, 2000, http://www.globalpolicy .org/component/content/article/221/47211.html.

2. Jan Lundberg, "Culture Change letter #100," *Culture Change*, June 18, 2005, http://www.culturechange.org/cms/index.php?option=com _content&task=view&id=6&Itemid=2.

3. David Zucchino, "Army Stage-Managed Fall of Hussein Statue," *Los Angeles Times*, July 3, 2004, http://articles.latimes.com/2004/ jul/03/nation/na-statue3.

4. Ellen Nakashima, "Travelers' Laptops May Be Detained At Border," *Washington Post*, August 1, 2008, http://www.washingtonpost.com/ wp-dyn/content/article/2008/08/01/AR2008080103030.html.

5. Robert Roy Britt, "14 Percent of U.S. Adults Can't Read," *Live Science*, January 10, 2009, http://www.livescience.com/culture/090110-illiterate-adults.html.

6. "U.S. Government Spending as Percent of GDP," http://www.usgovernmentspending.com/downchart_gs.php?year =1903_2010&view=1&expand=&units=p&fy=fy10&chart=G0-fed&bar=0&stack=1&size =m&title=US%20Government%20 Spending%20As%20Percent%20Of%20GDP&state=US&color =c&local=s.

7. Congressional Budget Office, "A Preliminary Analysis of the President's Budget and an Update of CBO's Budget and Economic Outlook," March 11, 2009, www.cbo.gov/ftpdocs/100xx/doc10014/ 03-20-PresidentBudget.pdf.

8. Edmund L. Andrews, "Wave of Debt Payments Facing U.S. Government," *New York Times*, November 22, 2009, http://www.nytimes .com/2009/11/23/business/23rates.html.

9. Louise Story and Eric Dash, "Banks Prepare for Big Bonuses, and Public Wrath," *New York Times*, January 9, 2010, http://www.nytimes.com/2010/01/10/business/10pay.html.

10. "Real Wages, 1947–2000," *Working Life*, http://www.workinglife.org/wiki/index.php?page=REAL+WAGES++1947-2000.

11. John Strachey, *The Theory and Practice of Socialism*, orig. 1936 (Hesperides Press, 2006), 28.

12. George Monbiot, "War on plastic bags is a waste of time," *Guardian*, April 16, 2009, http://www.guardian.co.uk/environment/georgemonbiot/2009/apr/15/plastic-bags-waste.

13. Richard Harris, "Global Warming is Irreversible, Study Says," National Public Radio, January, 26, 2009, http://www.npr.org/templates/story/story.php?storyId=99888903.

14. David Adam and agencies, "Russia's Armageddon plan to save Earth from collision with asteroid," *Guardian*, December 30, 2009, http://www.guardian.co.uk/world/2009/dec/30/russia-plan-save-earth-asteroid.

15. Dmitry Orlov, "Social Collapse Best Practices," Scribd Social Publishing Site, June 19, 2009, http://www.scribd.com/doc/16598076/Social-Collapse-Best-Practices-By-Dmitry-Orlov.

16. Arline T. Geronimus et al., "Excess Mortality among Blacks and Whites in the United States," *New England Journal of Medicine* 335, no. 21 (November 21, 1996): 1552–58, *http*://content.nejm.org/cgi/content/full/335/21/1552.

17. N. C. Aizenman, "New High In U.S. Prison Numbers," *Washington Post*, February 29, 2008, http://www.washingtonpost.com/wp-dyn/content/story/2008/02/28/ST2008022803016.html.

18. Justice Department, "Bureau of Justice Statistics, Total Correctional Population," Office of Justice Programs, http://bjs.ojp.usdoj.gov/index.cfm?ty=tp&tid=11.

19. Ed Pilkington, "US Prisons Hit New High: 1 in 100 Adults Jailed," *Guardian* (UK), March 1, 2008, http://www.guardian.co.uk/world/2008/mar/01/usa.

20. Mickey Z., "The world's worst polluter: U.S. military," *Online Journal*, August 14, 2009, http://onlinejournal.com/artman/publish/article_5014.shtml.

21. Steve Kretzmann, "A Climate of War," Oil Change International, http://priceofoil.org/climateofwar/.

22. Holman W. Jenkins, Jr., "Obama's Car Puzzle," *Wall Street Journal*, November, 12, 2008, http://online.wsj.com/article/ SB122645159441719325.html.

23. Crane Brinton, *The Anatomy of Revolution*, rev, ed. (New York: Vintage Books, 1965), 251.

24. David Grann, "Trial by Fire," *New Yorker*, September 7, 2009, http://www.newyorker.com/reporting/2009/09/07/090907fa _fact_grann.

25. Sandra Day O'Connor as quoted in Grann, "Trial by Fire."

26. Charles Duhigg, "Toxic Water: Clean Water Laws Are Neglected, at a Cost in Suffering," *New York Times*, September 12, 2009, http://www.nytimes.com/2009/09/13/us/13water.html?_r=1&pagewa nted=all.

27. Kenneth T. Walsh, "Obama's Secret Meeting with Historians," *U.S. News & World Report*, July 10, 2009, http://www.usnews.com/articles/ news/obama/2009/07/10/obamas-secret-meeting-with-historians.html.

28. Associated Press, "Chernobyl cover-up a catalyst for 'glasnost," MSNBC World News, April 24, 2006, http://www.msnbc.msn.com/ id/12403612.

29. Richard Lowry and Ramesh Ponnuru, "An Exceptional Debate," *National Review Online*, March 8, 2010, http://nrd.nationalreview .com/article/?q=M2FhMTg4NjkoNTQwMmFlMmYzZDg2YzgyYjdm YjhhMzU=.

30. "Box Cutters Found on Other September 11 Flights," CNN.com, September 24, 2001, http://archives.cnn.com/2001/US/09/23/ inv.investigation.terrorism/.

31. Dan Eggen, "9/11 Panel Suspected Deception by Pentagon," *Washington Post*, August 2, 2006, http://www.washingtonpost.com/ wp-dyn/content/article/2006/08/01/AR2006080101300.html.

32. Thomas H. Kean and Lee H. Hamilton, *Without Precedent: The Inside Story of the 9/11 Commission* (New York: Vintage Books, 2007), 257.

33. David Aaronovitch, "9/11 conspiracy theories: The truth is out there . . . just not on the internet," *Times Online*, April 29, 2009, http://women.timesonline.co.uk/tol/life_and_style/women/the_way _we_live/article6187493.ece.

34. Richard Cheney, "Richard Cheney: Saddam Hussein is a danger to world peace, from a speech to the Veterans of Foreign Wars by

America's Vice President, in Nashville," *Independent*, http://www.independent .co.uk/opinion/commentators/richard-cheney-saddam-hussein-is-a-danger-to-world-peace-641150.html.

35. Kent Conrad, "Senator Conrad's speech on Osama bin Laden and the war in Iraq," press release, March 29, 2004, http://conrad.senate .gov/pressroom/record.cfm?id=276812.

36. CNN Special Report Staff, "Bush to U.N.: We will not wait, U.S. sending more troops, ships to region," CNN.com/US, February 7, 2003, http://www.cnn.com/2003/US/02/06/sprj.irq.wrap/ index.html.

37. CNN Special Report Staff, "Bush:'Leave Iraq within 48 hours," CNN.com/US, March 17, 2003, http://www.cnn.com/2003/WORLD/ meast/03/17/sprj.irq.bush.transcript/ .

38. J. Scott Applewhite, "Bush: We'll find banned weapons in Iraq," *USAToday*, May 4, 2003, http://www.usatoday.com/news/world/ iraq/2003-05-03-bush-wmd_x.htm.

39. Frontline, "In Their Own Words: Who Said What When," *Frontline*, PBS.org, October 9, 2003, http://www.pbs.org/wgbh/pages/frontline/ shows/truth/why/said.html.

40. Fred Kaplan, "Vanishing Agents," *Slate*, May 30, 2003, http://www.slate.com/id/2083760.

41. Associated Press, "Wolfowitz comments revive doubts over Iraq's WMD," *USAToday*, June 1, 2003, http://www.usatoday.com/news/ world/iraq/2003-05-30-wolfowitz-iraq_x.htm.

42. Michelle Krupa, "Katrina's Displaced Worry about Census Count," *Times-Picayune*, July 25, 2009, http://www.nola.com/news/ index.ssf/2009/07/katrinas_displaced_worry_about.html.

43. Valerie Martin, "Zeitoun by Dave Eggers," *Guardian*, March 21, 2010, http://www.guardian.co.uk/books/2010/mar/21/zeitoun-dave-eggers-book-review.

44. Campbell Robertson, "Justice Department to Review New Orleans's Troubled Police Force," *New York Times*, May 17, 2010, http://www.nytimes.com/2010/05/18/us/18orleans.html.

45. Ben Ehrenreich, "Why Did We Focus on Securing Haiti Rather Than Helping Haitians?" *Slate*, January 21, 2010, http://www.slate.com/ id/2242078.

46. Marcus Mabry, "Eye of the Political Storm," *Newsweek/MSNBC.com*, September 10, 2005, http://www.msnbc.msn.com/id/9280375/ site/newsweek/page/2/.

47. Wendell Goler, Molly Henneberg, and the Associated Press, "Bush Visits Katrina Recovery Volunteers on Gulf Coast Trip," Fox News.com, April 27, 2006, http://www.foxnews.com/story/ 0,2933,193425,00.html.

48. Bryan Walsh, "Green Jobs: Still More Promise Than Reality," Time.com, http://www.time.com/time/health/article/ 0,8599,1883702,00.html.

49. Associated Press, "U.S. Ranks Just 42nd in Life Expectancy," August 11, 2007, http://www.msnbc.msn.com/id/20228552/.

50. Tom Raum, Associated Press, "Obama Refocuses on Jobs After Weak Labor Report," *Journal Gazette* (Fort Wayne, IN), January 8, 2010, http://www.journalgazette.net/article/20100108/APW/1001081540.

51. Chris Hedges, "Ralph Nader Was Right About Barack Obama," *Truthdig*, March 1, 2010, http://www.truthdig.com/report/print/ ralph_nader_was_right_about_barack_obama_20100301/.

52. Robert Reich, "The Enthusiasm Gap," *Huffington Post*, February 28, 2010, http://www.huffingtonpost.com/robert-reich/the-enthusiasm-gap_b_479981.html.

53. Ibid.

54. The website's URL is http://www.shadowstats.com.

55. As quoted in Husna Haq, "Who's Poor in America? US Tweaks How it Defines Poverty," *Christian Science Monitor*, March 3, 2010, http://www.csmonitor.com/USA/2010/0303/Who-s-poor-in-America-US-tweaks-how-it-defines-poverty.

56. Mark Guarino, "ABB shooting: Economy may play role in workplace violence," MinnPost.com, January 8, 2010, http://www.minnpost .com/worldcsm/2010/01/08/14797/abb_shooting_economy_may _play_role_in_workplace_violence.

57. Holly Watt, "Violent Crime Fell in 2007 from Previous Year," *Washington Post*, September 16, 2008, http://www.washingtonpost .com/wp-dyn/content/article/2008/09/15/AR2008091503079.html.

58. Jeremy Hobson, "Working, but dissatisfied," Marketplace from American Public Media, March 4, 2010, http://marketplace .publicradio.org/display/web/2010/03/04/pm-dissatisfied-workers.

59. Joe Weisenthal, "The Insane Manifesto of Austin Crash Pilot Joseph Andrew Stack," *Business Insider*, February 18, 2010, http://www.businessinsider.com/joseph-andrew-stacks-insane-manifesto-2010-2.

60. Stephen Spruiell, "National Review: Politics of the Austin Crash," NPR.org, February 19, 2010, http://www.npr.org/templates/story/story.php?storyId=123882009.

61. Ted Anthony and Mary Foster, Associated Press, "Latest Fix Failure Dampens Spirits," *Herald-Sun* (Durham, NC), May 31, 2010, http://www.heraldsun.com/view/full_story/7750860/article-Latest-fix-failure-dampens-spirits?instance=most_commented.

62. "Just 53% Say Capitalism Better Than Socialism," April 9, 2009, http://www.rasmussenreports.com/public_content/politics/general_politics/april_2009/just_53_say_capitalism_better_than_socialism.

63. Ibid.

64. Stephe Kotkin, "Minding the Inequality Gap," *New York Times*, October 4, 2008, http://www.nytimes.com/2008/10/05/business/05shelf.html.

65. Monica Lewiston, reader comment, *New York Times*, September 1, 2009, http://community.nytimes.com/comments/www.nytimes.com/2009/09/01/opinion/01herbert.html.

66. William Haboush, reader comment, *New York Times*, September 1, 2009, http://community.nytimes.com/comments/www.nytimes.com/2009/09/01/opinion/01herbert.html.

67. Dave, reader comment, *New York Times*, September 13, 2009, http://community.nytimes.com/comments/www.nytimes.com/2009/09/13/us/13water.html?sort=oldest&offset=2.

68. Economic Affairs Bureau, "Gumption to organize?," *Dollars & Sense*, May 1, 2009, http://www.amazon.com/Gumption-organize-strategies-management-Editorial/dp/B00342N8QE.

69. Human Rights Watch, "US: Respect Rights of Child Detainees in Iraq," May 19, 2008, http://www.hrw.org/en/news/2008/05/19/us-respect-rights-child-detainees-iraq.

70. Scott Tobias, "Michael Moore," interview, A. V. Club, *Onion*, October 2, 2009, http://www.avclub.com/articles/michael-moore,33624/.

71. Sewell Chan, "A Trove of N.Y.P.D. Surveillance Files," *New York Times*, May 16, 2007, http://empirezone.blogs.nytimes.com/2007/05/16/a-trove-of-nypd-surveillance-files/?scp=1-b&sq=A+Nov.+

13%2C+2003+digest+noting+the+Web+site+of+the+editorial+cartoon
ist+and+activist+Ted+Rall&st=nyt.

72. James Adler, letter to the editor, *New York Times*, December 12, 2009.

73. Margaret Wente, "Copenhagen Climate Rage: Who's the Villain?"
Globe and Mail, December 9, 2009, http://vi.theglobeandmail.com/
servlet/story/RTGAM.20091209.escenic_1395002/BNStory/Other/
MARGARET+WENTE.

74. Amrith Lal, "Need to look beyond capitalism," *Times of India*,
November 24, 2009, http://timesofindia.indiatimes.com/
articleshow/articleshow/5261695.cms.

75. Don Lee, "Job Market Worsens for Recent College Graduates," *Los
Angeles Times*, December 14, 2009, http://mobile.latimes.com/inf/
infomo?view=webarticle&feed:a=latimes_1min&feed:c=topstories&fe
ed:i=51064243&nopaging=1.

76. Oxford Analytica, "Mass Unemployment Escalates," *Forbes*, March 5,
2009, http://www.forbes.com/2009/03/04/unemployment-europe-
economy-business_oxford.html.

77. Kathy Mcafee and Myrna Wood, "What is the Revolutionary Potential
of Women's Liberation?," Women's Liberation Movement, On-line
Archival Collection, Special Collections Library, Duke University,
April 1997, http://scriptorium.lib.duke.edu/wlm/mcafee.

78. Emmanuel Saez, "Striking it Richer: The Evolution of Top Incomes
in the United States," updated August 2009, http://www.econ
.berkeley.edu/~saez.

79. Tim Rutten, "A Snapshot of Income Disparity," *Los Angeles Times*,
February 24, 2010, http://articles.latimes.com/2010/feb/24/
opinion/la-oe-rutten24-2010feb24.

80. Frank Newport, "Americans: Economy Takes Precedence Over
Environment," Gallup, March 19, 2009, http://www.gallup.com/
poll/116962/americans-economy-takes-precedence-environment.aspx.

81. Pew Research Center, "Inside the Middle Class: Bad Time Hit the
Good Life," survey report, April 9, 2008, http://pewsocialtrends.org/
assets/pdf/MC-Middle-class-report.pdf.

82. Edmund L. Andrews and Peter Baker, "A.I.G. Planning Huge Bonuses
After $170 Billion Bailout," *New York Times*, March 14, 2009,
http://www.nytimes.com/2009/03/15/business/15AIG.html?_r=2.

83. Rasmussen Reports, "66% Angry at Government Policies, 60% Say
Neither Party Has Answers," survey report, September 22, 2009,

http://www.rasmussenreports.com/public_content/politics/general_politics/september_2009/66_angry_at_government_policies_60_say_neither_party_has_answers.

84. Brian Montopoli, "Police Prepare For Possible Election Night Riots," CBSNews.com, October 22, 2008, http://www.cbsnews.com/8301-502163_162-4539330-502163.html.

85. Paul Reynolds, "Eyewitness: The Battle of Seattle," BBC News Online, December 2, 1999, http://news.bbc.co.uk/2/hi/547581.stm.

86. Jim Lobe, Inter Press Service, "The Truth, the Whole Truth and Nothing But . . ." *Asia Times Online*, June 4, 2003, http://www.atimes.com/atimes/Middle_East/EF04Ak02.html.

87. Don Monkerud, "US Income Inequality Continues to Grow," *Common Dreams*, July 17, 2009, http://www.commondreams.org/view/ 2009/07/17-8.

88. Ibid.

89. Don Monkerud, "US Income Inequality Continues to Grow," Information Clearing House, July 18, 2009, http://www.informationclearinghouse .info/article23094.htm.

90. Jack Hough, "True or False: U.S. Economic Stats Lie," SmartMoney.com, June 8, 2009, http://www.smartmoney.com/investing/stocks/true-or-false-u-s-economic-stats-lie.

91. See the entire Failed States Index 2010 at http://www.foreignpolicy .com/articles/2010/06/21/the_failed_states_index_2010.

92. "Feature Transcript: Part 2," The Corporation, November 13, 2006, http://www.hellocoolworld.com/files/TheCorporation/Transcript _finalpt2%20copy.pdf.

93. The Editors, "A Turning Point for Eminent Domain?" *New York Times*, November 12, 2009, http://roomfordebate.blogs.nytimes .com/2009/ 11/12/a-turning-point-for-eminent-domain.

94. Tibor Machan, "Must Corporations Be in Bed with Government?" FreedomPolitics.com, October 5, 2009, http://www.freedompolitics .com/articles/government-1643-system-corporations.html.

95. Sharon Weinberger, "Report: U.S. is World's Top Arms Seller, Again," *Wired*, September 10, 2009, http://www.wired.com/dangerroom/2009/09/report-us-is-worlds-biggest-arms-seller-again/.

96. Joel Blocker, "Western Press Review: Russia's Prospects, OPEC's Decision," Radio Free Europe, Radio Liberty, March 3, 2000, http://www.rferl .org/content/article/1093640.html.

97. V. I. Lenin, *The Defeat of Russia and the Revolutionary Crisis*, ed. D. Walters and R. Cymbala, 2005, http://www.marxists.org/archive/lenin/works/1915/sep/x01.htm.

98. Paul Steinhauser, "Don't Investigate Torture Techniques," Politics blog, CNN, May 6, 2009, http://politicalticker.blogs.cnn.com/2009/05/06/poll-dont-investigate-torture-techniques/?fbid=NcBdPTL48Qv.

99. Challenger, Gray & Christmas, Inc., "Challenger Corporate Cost-Cutting Survey," survey report, January 26, 2009, http://www.challengergray.com/press/Cost%20Cutting%20Survey.pdf.

100. Ellen Barry, "Russian Dissident's Passion Endures Despite Tests," *New York Times*, January 11, 2010, http://www.nytimes.com/2010/01/12/world/europe/12dissident.html.

101. Geoffrey D. Garin, "Celebrating the Revolutionary Party," *Harvard Crimson*, December 15, 1973, http://www.thecrimson.com/article/1973/12/15/celebrating-the-revolutionary-party-pbtbomorrow-is/.

102. James F. Jarboe, "The Threat of Eco-Terrorism," Federal Bureau of Investigation, February 12, 2002, http://www.fbi.gov/congress/congress02/jarboe021202.htm.

103. Kevin Bohn, "Gun Sales Surge After Obama's Election," CNN.com, November 11, 2008, http://edition.cnn.com/2008/CRIME/11/11/obama.gun.sales/.

104. Mark Potok, Southern Poverty Law Center, "Rage on the Right," *Intelligence Report* 137 (Spring 2010), http://www.splcenter.org/get-informed/intelligence-report/browse-all-issues/2010/spring/rage-on-the-right.

105. Rush Limbaugh, "Obama Report on 'Right-Wing Radicals' Timed for Tea Paries," transcript, April 14, 2009, http://www.rushlimbaugh.com/home/daily/site_041409/content/01125108.guest.html.

106. Dragonfly_Path (Online Poster), "To everyone who believes the 'government' is taking away our constitutional rights . . ." SodaHead.com, March 20, 2010, http://www.sodahead.com/united-states/to-everyone-who-believes-the-government-is-taking-away-our-constitutional-rights/question-922733/.

107. James Baker, "Florida Recount," radio interview transcript, *NewsHour with Jim Lehrer*, November 10, 2000, http://www.pbs.org/newshour/bb/election/july-dec00/florida_11-10.html.

108. Office of Intelligence and Analysis, "Rightwing Extremism: Current Economic and Political Climate Fueling Resurgence in Radicalization and Recruitment," report, April 7, 2009, http://www.fas.org/irp/eprint/rightwing.pdf.

109. Human Rights First, "2008 Hate Crime Survey: USA," http://www.humanrightsfirst.org/discrimination/reports.aspx?s=usa&p=violent-hate-crimes-on-the-rise.

110. Anneli Rufus, "Who Are We to Judge?" Stuck blog, *Psychology Today*, May 14, 2009, http://www.psychologytoday.com/blog/stuck/200905/who-are-we-judge.

111. Marina Margaret Heiss, "Introverted iNtuitive Thinking Judging," TypeLogic.com, October 17, 2009, http://typelogic.com/intj.html.

112. Jessica Ravitz, "Airport Security Bares All, or Does It?" CNN.com, May 18, 2009, http://edition.cnn.com/2009/TRAVEL/05/18/airport.security.body.scans/index.html.

113. Scott Shane, "Shadow of 9/11 is Cast Again," *New York Times*, December 30, 2009, http://www.nytimes.com/2009/12/31/us/31intel.html.

114. Ibid.

115. Howard J. Ehrlich, ed., *Reinventing Anarchy, Again* (San Francisco: AK Press, 1996), 65.

116. Bootie Cosgrove-Mather, "Creationism Trumps Evolution," poll report, CBS News, November 22, 2004, http://www.cbsnews.com/stories/2004/11/22/opinion/polls/main657083.shtml

117. Peter Gelderloos, *How Nonviolence Protects the State* (New York: South End Press, 2007).

118. Jean-Paul Sartre, *Notebooks for an Ethics* (Chicago: University of Chicago Press, 1992), 263.

ABOUT THE AUTHOR

A Pulitzer Prize finalist and twice the winner of the Robert F. Kennedy Journalism Award, TED RALL is a syndicated political cartoonist, opinion columnist, graphic novelist, and occasional war correspondent whose work has appeared in hundreds of publications, including the *New York Times*, the *Washington Post*, the *Village Voice*, and the *Los Angeles Times*.

ABOUT SEVEN STORIES PRESS

SEVEN STORIES PRESS is an independent book publisher based in New York City, with distribution throughout the United States, Canada, England, and Australia. We publish works of the imagination by such writers as Nelson Algren, Russell Banks, Octavia E. Butler, Ani DiFranco, Assia Djebar, Ariel Dorfman, Coco Fusco, Barry Gifford, Hwang Sok-yong, Lee Stringer, and Kurt Vonnegut, to name a few, together with political titles by voices of conscience, including the Boston Women's Health Collective, Noam Chomsky, Angela Y. Davis, Human Rights Watch, Derrick Jensen, Ralph Nader, Gary Null, Project Censored, Barbara Seaman, Gary Webb, and Howard Zinn, among many others. Seven Stories Press believes publishers have a special responsibility to defend free speech and human rights, and to celebrate the gifts of the human imagination, wherever we can. For additional information, visit www.sevenstories.com.